Bereave

Bereavement at Work

A Practical Guide

David Charles-Edwards

Duckworth

First published in 2000 by
Gerald Duckworth & Co. Ltd.
61 Frith Street, London W1V 5TA
Tel: 0207 434 4242
Fax: 0207 434 4420
Email: enquiries@duckworth-publishers.co.uk
www.ducknet.co.uk

A catalogue record for this book is available
from the British Library

ISBN 0 7156 2861 5

Typeset by Derek Doyle & Associates, Liverpool
Printed in Great Britain by
Redwood Books Ltd, Trowbridge

Contents

For Samuel, Owen, Rosa
and Maya.

Foreword

Ten years ago, after the New Year break, I returned to work to discover that a close colleague's son had been killed in a road accident in the early hours of New Year's morning. He'd had a row with his father, picked up the car keys and drove off, never to return. The sense of personal devastation was colossal, almost too big to look square in the eye. As his boss and a member of the family who owned the business, I felt an enormous sense of duty and sympathy towards him, but a great lack of personal skill to express these adequately. I am not alone, I fear. Many managers and leaders of businesses are great at the hard skills of managing performance and do their level best when it comes to coping with the special challenges posed when colleagues at work suffer personal difficulty. In the case of death, though, we are often found wanting at the time we are most needed.

David Charles-Edwards's book provides a crutch for all of us who want to help but don't know the 'right' way to do it. His cogent and detailed descriptions of the underlying patterns associated with bereavement at work are dealt with in accessible language and contain vivid accounts of real life experiences. It is a practical guide for what has for too long been a taboo subject.

Ross Warburton, Chairman, Warburtons Limited

Acknowledgements

I would like to acknowledge in particular Peter Twist, formerly of the Metropolitan Police, and Alison, my wife, for their supportive and challenging help.

Thanks also to Simon Burne, Ashley Callaghan, John Crace, Debbie Collins, Maureen Hanson, Tam Kearney, Annie and Titus Mercer, Bill Merrington, Sue and Tony Pasternak, Tim Pears, Graham Powell, Judyann Roblee, Wendy Robinson, Hugh Scurfield, Anna Thomas and Richard Worsley for the various ways they have influenced what I think and feel about death, bereavement and work.

I also want to thank Ross Warburton and Dr Robert Abbott of Warburtons Limited, Colin Parry of the Warrington Project, Kay Walker of Loros The Leicestershire Hospice and Simon Armson and Norman Keir of the Samaritans, for varied support. John Flouch gave me great encouragement in writing the booklet published by CEPEC, to which this is a successor, and to Robin Baird-Smith and Martin Rynja of Duckworth in guiding me towards the present edition.

All of these people have contributed, directly or indirectly, to this book, but none, however, can share with me responsibility for its deficiencies.

The Warrington Project

I would like to honour the many innocents slaughtered needlessly in Northern Ireland and Britain by terrorists, including Tim Parry and Johnathan Ball killed by an IRA bomb in Warrington on 20 March 1993.

The Warrington Project is dedicated to their memory.

About the Author

David Charles-Edwards is a management consultant specialising in leadership, team building and counselling skills at work. He is also part-time Anglican priest-in-charge of Clifton and Newton, near Rugby. He is married to Alison and they have two sons, Owen and Samuel. His first wife, Janet, died in 1966: they had one daughter, Anna.

David formerly managed the British Association for Counselling, before which he headed the new NHS personnel functions, first in Hackney in London and then in Oxfordshire. His earlier work experience included being a national serviceman in the Royal Artillery, a temporary Prison Officer at HMP, Pentonville, a curate in Putney, south London, a marketing researcher with the Metal Box Company and an adviser with The Industrial Society.

His counselling experience includes training in re-evaluation counselling and in relationship counselling with Relate. He was educated at Westminster School, Trinity College, Cambridge, and Lincoln Theological College.

1

Is It Any of Our Business?

- 'Least said, soonest mended'
- Emotional Literacy and Leadership
- Loss, Change and Transition
- Barriers Breaking Down between Work and Personal Life
- Support and Motivation

'Least said, soonest mended'

At least 500 years ago the proverb was coined 'Neither for peace nor for warre, will a dead Bee gather honey'. In the hive, a bee's remains are meticulously removed, so that there is no 'dead space', and then they are discarded. Likewise, in terms of output, the dead employee is unproductive. If the deceased is the partner, parent or child of one of our colleagues – they can be of no further use to the company as a staff supporter or motivator. 'Let the dead bury their dead', Jesus is reported to have said. That life is for living and for the living is a principle followed in the natural world, where many animals quickly ignore the corpse of a member of their own family, unless it is regarded as edible. There are, however, exceptions: elephants have been seen staying with the body of a member of their family group and engaging in behaviour that looks to human eyes very like a bereavement ritual.

If we concentrate on the bottom line, it might seem that we should cut our losses, or at least minimise any further investment, human or financial, for the dying and bereaved. Pension and insurance arrangements and an adequate compassionate leave policy should cover it; with a note of sympathy, a floral tribute or contribution to a chosen charity and perhaps attendance at the funeral.

The resource implications of doing more may be greater than we first imagine: according to CRUSE, the bereavement care agency, about 3,500 people are newly bereaved in the UK each day and one person is widowed every three minutes.

Grieving is not necessarily open to a quick fix. The bereaved often need ongoing thoughtful support over a period of weeks or months, rather than days. For some people, the feelings associated with death are embarrassing, and can cause us to feel uncomfortable. Bereavement can undermine years of conditioning in the British stiff upper lip. Hence the need for tight control. No wonder Geoffrey Gorer in his study *Death, Grief and Mourning* (1965) concluded that 'giving way to grief is stigmatised as morbid, unhealthy, demoralising. The proper action of a friend and well-wisher is felt to be the distraction of a mourner from his or her grief'. Thirty years after that was written such an attitude is still widespread, even though a more enlightened and open attitude is becoming more common.

Whereas sex was the great taboo for the Victorians, for much of the 20th century it was replaced by death. Sex has often been promoted to symbolise health, happiness, eternal youth and success in our culture. Death, on the other hand, can be seen as representing the opposite of life, as well as being one of the realities that is most dreaded, despite or perhaps because of its inevitability. No wonder that it is seen as negative, depressing or demoralising and not felt to be an acceptable subject for general discussion.

Emotional Literacy and Leadership

Attitudes are, however, changing. This is part of a broader recognition of the importance of emotional intelligence at work replacing the idea that feelings and intelligence are opposites and almost mutually exclusive. That approach saw feelings as largely out of place at work, because they stopped people thinking clearly and logically. Hence, a culture was encouraged in which the acknowledgement and expression of feelings, especially among men, was restricted as far as possible to home. This started at school and continued at work, from the armed services to factories and offices through to hospitals. The old stereotype that men are unemotional and intelligent and women are the opposite is under concerted attack in the face of evidence as opposed to prejudice. Sport was something of a half way house in which boys and men were allowed an outlet for their passion and exuberance: that trend gathers apace. The handshakes and smiles of yesterday are replaced today by the hugs and whoops of triumph when the goal is scored, the wicket taken. This is endorsed by enlightened coaches, who know that enthusiasm, passion and commitment can be increased by their expression. Of course there are still many, in sport, parenting and teaching as well as in the workplace, who sing to a different tune: all stick and minimum carrot. 'Don't waste time and breath, conserve it for the essential task of showing them where they have got it wrong'. Good managers, as part of their responsibility for motivation, realise how important it is to encourage and praise their staff not only for achievements but also for effort.

There seem to be five interrelated strands of thought behind these changing attitudes:

- Feelings are closely related to the energy, enthusiasm and motivation (or the lack of them) needed at work.
- Within feelings and intuition, there may be important information that a business is unwise to ignore.
- Emotional intelligence is often an essential ingredient for building good working relationships with internal and external customers.
- Feelings are part of our humanity and deserve to be valued, as well as managed, rather than belittled.
- Human character traits traditionally associated with women are less likely to be discounted now as a result of changing attitudes in society towards women.

People at work who are comfortable with their feelings and those of other people are more likely to respect and be interested in the feelings that are associated with bereavement and affect behaviour and performance.

Loss, Change and Transition

For a business to prosper, it is crucial that change is managed effectively. To do that, people are needed who can cope with transition at all levels, including the personal.

Most change involves both loss and gain. The ultimate losses are those of our own life or the lives of those closest to us. Consequently, the ability to cope with the death of others may well help us to manage other lesser losses, including those at work. Conversely, unresolved loss in one area of our life may make subsequent changes difficult to manage, even where the link between the two may not be obvious.

Colin Maxwell (1989) wrote that 'The Jungian view of growth through loss has great relevance in terms of bereavement in the workplace. It offers an ideal opportunity for organisations to demonstrate their caring style of management. Bereavement more than anything else is able to cut through social and organisational barriers – through custom and practice. It reminds us of our common humanity and makes the differences between us seem irrelevant and superficial'. A caring style of management may still sound sentimental to some, but it need not be. It is rather a passionate commitment to the task and to the people. If the company does not care about me, why should I care about the success of the company?

> Peter, a 43-year-old sales manager, was made redundant in October. He was a resilient person who had responded positively and enthusiastically to change in the company over the years, seeing it as a challenge. His senior management predicted that he would cope well with the redundancy: he was one of many and therefore need not take it personally, and his prospects for re-employment were excellent because of his good reputation and contacts. But his employers had not taken into account the implications of a double bereavement: his mother had died four months before and his wife a year previously. At the time, he had apparently taken their deaths 'amazingly well, considering' and had carried on 'almost as if nothing had happened'. The culture in the company did little to encourage the grieving process. Redundancy was the last straw. It felt to him as if his world, already crumbling, had finally crashed. Before he could give his attention to the job search, he had to attend to his grief and begin to reconstruct a world in which going for a job made some kind of sense.

In Peter's case, he had some bereavement counselling, which concentrated on the deaths of the two most important women in his life. After a few sessions he was able to refocus on the job search successfully and function effectively at interviews. His resources had virtually run dry by the time the redundancy occurred. If he had been made redundant before the bereavements, he would have probably taken it in his stride.

As children we sometimes have two perceptions of the world: one, a sense that we will never die; the other, a feeling that the world about us does not or should not change. Both attitudes usually change with age, but their echoes can linger in nostalgia. As a consequence, we can feel resentful if our organisation does not keep things as they are or used to be, even though adult realism indicates that the world is in a constant state of flux, as we are, that companies which do not adapt, perish.

We need to recognise and come to terms with this tension, learning to accept and even, where appropriate, to welcome change. This is preferable to trying to block it, like someone who tries to fight the ageing process instead of growing old gracefully. The death of someone close to us is about the most challenging change some people are ever likely to face.

Barriers Breaking Down between Work and Personal Life

Erecting mental barriers between our personal and work lives is a common way of managing both. At work, we may get respite from family pressures and vice versa. We need to let our concerns in one area go, so that we can concentrate on the other. These intrinsically useful barriers may, however, be negatively reinforced if people at work are treated as if their life outside work neither existed nor mattered. A way of coping with this situation is to try and split life into two: at work being whole-hearted about the job, but at home being all for the family and 'never the twain shall meet'.

But the whole person is there in both aspects of our life, notably in our capacity to learn, develop, and mature. When it comes to death and dying, the connection between the public and the private, between work and non-work, a rigid split becomes particularly difficult to sustain. The impact of the experience makes it often difficult to draw a line around it, even though the bereaved person may want to use work to try and forget a little.

A good employer does not reinforce the split between life at work and life outside work, because they will intrude on each other. Successes and significant events, such as births as well as deaths, need to be recognised and, where appropriate, allowed for.

Support and Motivation

Those who are helped to work through a bereavement are more likely to be able to give support to colleagues who face major difficulties. On the other hand, if bereavement has not been adequately dealt with, there may be continuing problems in an individual's relationship to work. These can include, for example, lack of concentration, reduced interest and motivation, depression, displaced anger and irritability.

A common response to a bereavement is that it is a time 'when you find out who your real friends are'. These are the people who not only care but who also, through their skills and sensitivity, avoid 'putting their foot in it'. A bereaved person is exceptionally vulnerable and, in a state of heightened awareness, can be simultaneously both appreciative and also critical of other people's responses. He or she may view other people in the extreme as either good or bad. If others are experienced as a source of help rather than hindrance, long-term goodwill has been won and the ripples from that will have a positive impact on other employees who observe, maybe discreetly, how a colleague was treated at such a time.

> The young wife of Colin, a market researcher in a packaging company, died after a protracted battle against a malignant disease. The personal support of his departmental head was crucial to his recovery. He gave Colin time to talk through how things were going and reassured him that he need not worry about work at such a time. The concern continued to be expressed for months, thus making him feel that he was not under pressure to 'pull his socks up quickly' and to behave 'as if nothing had happened'. The support which that manager (and through him the company) had given at such a traumatic time in his life strengthened Colin's loyalty and commitment to them both.

Goodwill can thus reach beyond the person immediately affected. This is true, whether the employee is dying or is bereaved. Others will draw their own conclusions about the quality of support (or lack of it) which they and their families might receive in such a crisis themselves. Does the organisation communicate a concern through its managers about staff as human beings rather than just as a pair of hands or a unit of production? An organisation's support needs to flow from a total 'quality' commitment to staff, rather than from seeing people merely as instruments for exploitation and securing profits. These messages flow out of the company to customers and even suppliers. A concern for ethical investment includes how staff are treated, wherever the company operates. It is no use having a framed Investors in People certificate in reception, if the organisation is experienced as callous, incompetent and insensitive when staff or clients are at their most vulnerable.

The case for the company to provide committed, informed

support can therefore be justified on a variety of grounds. In this book we will consider what that commitment might involve in practice.

2

How the Organisation Can Help

- Organisational Culture and Core Values
- Compassionate Leave Policy
- Payment of Benefits Following Death
- Carers
- Induction and Training
- A Company Focal Point
- Bereavement Counselling

The employer has a significant role in the bereavement process:

- – in representing part of wider society;
- – in providing a context for mourning;
- – sometimes in providing an escape from grieving;
- – in being a bridge between grief and returning to 'normality'.

Organisational Culture and Core Values

The experience of bereavement or terminal illness often concentrates the mind on what is really important. The need to feel that work is of value to society as well as a means of making money often comes to the fore in answer to the question: why bother? Of course, even the most inspiring work can be reduced to drudgery by the touch of death. The sense that the organisation cares about its people, customers and staff, and not just about success, however that may be measured, is important at such a time.

Many organisations find benefit in reviewing and revising their core values and management style. With a range of pressures on companies to become less bureaucratic and rigid, corporate values and style tend to replace explicit rules and policies as a more flexible way of holding the company together and giving it an identity. If the values are thought to be just bits of paper that do not reflect how people really try to behave, especially those at the top, the result is cynicism and a belief that the company is hypocritical. In that case the end result is counter-productive.

On the other hand, a strong sense of a shared direction can help raise morale and promote motivation: 'A vision without a task is a dream: a task without a vision is drudgery'. Good values need to be promoted with determination, and checked out with good listening and other mechanisms, such as staff attitude surveys or upward feedback. An enlightened organisation is also one in which people can be themselves, take risks and be messengers of bad as well as good news without fear. Those characteristics of not having to pretend can help the business face up to and address problems, rather than ignoring them until it is too late. They can also help create a climate in which it feels relatively safe to be vulnerable personally as well as professionally.

The Industrial Society[1] has put the relationship between the different terms as follows:

- A *Vision* is our ultimate aim.
- The *Mission* is the purpose for which we exist.
- Our core *Values* are the beliefs which we hold that guide our day-to-day behaviour, actions and decisions.

The atmosphere of a workplace has been described as a very subtle group presence. John O'Donoghue wrote that 'It is difficult to describe or analyse an ethos; yet you immediately sense its power and effect. Where it is positive, wonderful things can happen. It is a joy to come to work, because the atmosphere comes out to meet you, and it is a happy atmosphere. It is caring, kind and creative. Where the ethos of the workplace is negative and destructive, people wake up in the morning and the first thought of going to work literally makes them ill.'[2] Many workplaces fall somewhere in between, depending on events and personalities as well as the attitudes that trickle down from directors and managers at every level.

A positive atmosphere does not preclude conflict or anger, but it does enable people to be managed constructively. Conflict can be managed more or less constructively and anger channelled so that abuse and bullying are minimised if not avoided. Enlightened leaders, from chief executives to first line managers and supervisors, appreciate that it is part of their job to help create such an atmosphere. To do so requires skill as well as commitment, but is an important ingredient in developing people who are motivated and focused.

With respect to death and bereavement, a supportive, enabling organisational culture is inevitably more appropriate in helping staff cope with bereavement than is a blaming, punitive one. The most relevant value guiding day-to-day behaviour is that of mutual respect for people irrespective of their status or seniority. (This is discussed more fully in the Core Conditions of Helping in Appendix 1.)

Aspects of an organisational approach helpful in supporting people at work to cope with bereavement or terminal illness include:

- an unequivocal commitment to staff as a resource rather than a cost even if during bereavement they are less productive than usual;
- a commitment to support employees during bereavement, recognising that bereaved staff who are well supported by their employer and subsequently work through their grief well, will invariably grow in the process and strengthen their loyalty to the company;
- a commitment to people in the whole of their lives, recognising that the quality of life outside work is relevant to their contribution at work;

And a company culture in which:

- it is acceptable to have 'off' days;
- open and honest communication is encouraged;
- the difference between direct feedback and attacking colleagues is understood;
- bullying, abuse and inappropriate fear is unacceptable;[3] [4]
- human vulnerability is respected, not despised as weakness;
- feelings and their expression, including tears, are seen as part of our humanity rather than merely a cause of embarrassment;
- a management style is promoted, which takes account of the human needs of and pressures on staff (and their families).

Compassionate Leave Policy

Compassionate leave policy needs to be flexible and generous, with the line manager having a delegated discretion to offer more than the minimum if it seems warranted. Compassionate leave should be available over a period and not restricted to the time before and immediately after the funeral. It may also be relevant during a person's terminal illness and not only after they have died.

> In the Young Offenders Unit, the inmates could only have compassionate leave to attend the funeral in the case of parents or siblings, not for grandparents, who in some cases happened to be the adults to whom they were closest. An imaginative chaplain offered a parallel service in the chapel at the same time as the funeral.

A family can be defined as those you care for and who care for you and compassionate leave is increasingly encompassed under the broader heading of Family Leave. This will include parental, maternal and paternal, and adoption leave as well as a more general heading of leave for family reasons. Under the latter heading, the TUC includes death and such other pressing reasons as the illness of a spouse, elderly relative, child or person looking after a child, a child's wedding, as well as caring for partners, dependants and individuals in stable relationships though not related by marriage or blood.[5]

Organisations vary, as the examples below illustrate, as to how prescriptive they are. In the first example, a close relative could be interpreted narrowly or more flexibly to include an unmarried partner, gay or straight, or even a very close friend. Companies attempting a detailed list need to include unmarried partners in this day and age if they are serious about their commitment to equality of employment in all its practices, policies and procedures.

Neither example mentions specifically the death of colleagues, even though a number of staff would be expected to attend the funeral in such an event, and it would normally take place during working hours.

Examples of company policy in relation to bereavement

Example 1. *Time off: introductory comments*

> If urgent private matters require your attention at any time, you should apply for leave of absence to your senior. Such requests are always considered sympathetically. Management will generally be tolerant regarding requests for occasional days off (normally without pay) for family reasons and a more disciplined approach towards other personal business which can normally be arranged on pre-arranged 'days off'. It is essential that you give as much notice as possible.

Example 2. *Bereavement*

Where an employee is personally responsible for the funeral arrangements of a close relative, up to three days' leave may be granted with pay. This will only apply at the time of the bereavement, however, and is restricted to close relatives.

Example 3. *Bereavement leave*

An employee is eligible for up to three days' leave with pay in respect of the death of an immediate relative or dependant, who is defined as spouse, son, daughter, parent, brother, sister and also includes a common-law spouse and legally adopted children. In the event of the death of a grandparent, grandchild or an in-law, the employee may be granted paid leave to attend the funeral.

Example 4. *Leave of absence to attend funerals of near relatives*

Leave with pay, normally not exceeding one day, will be granted to members of the staff to enable them to attend the funeral of a wife or husband, child, father, mother, step-father, step-mother, brother, sister, step-brother, step-sister, mother-in-law, father-in-law, grandfather and grandmother, and their spouses. In the case of other near-relatives, staff will be allowed to change their turn of duty, where practicable, to enable them to attend the funeral.

The Company has indicated that when an employee is the sole member of the family responsible for making all the arrangements in connection with the funeral, the local manager can, at his or her discretion, grant leave with pay up to a total of five days, if considered necessary.

A large national utility also provided its staff with a list as a guideline, which included a number of relatives, which are omitted from the third example above. These are grandchildren, brother-in-law, sister-in-law, son-in-law and daughter-in-law. In this organisation, for some of these categories, paid leave for a funeral was only to be granted if the relative shared the same house as the staff member. Lists can be helpful, but also woefully inadequate to deal with the complex reality of human relationships. That is why guidelines rather than rigid rules fit the bill best.

Time off to attend funerals in work time is sometimes given to attend any funeral, particularly for those of former colleagues, without requiring the member of staff to take annual leave. But this is seldom laid down as company policy and is considered as discretionary.

While there are stories about the employee who goes to an

impossible number of grandmothers' funerals, a caring manager who asks sensitively about the deceased will come to realise how emotionally close the person is to the one who has died. It is the level of emotional closeness, rather than the formal relationship, that generally determines the level of mourning the staff member will experience.

Payment of Benefits Following Death

The prompt payment of benefits, including shares, to the person the employee has specified can be difficult if no specification has been made. Companies try to ensure that such payments go to the right person, especially dependants, such as a partner and children, including adopted ones, who are under the age of 18 or still receiving full-time education or training. Where there is a dispute or lack of clarity about who is entitled to receive benefits, the employer needs to consult the person's legal representative.

Carers

A much bigger challenge for organisations arises in the case of long-term sickness of someone in a close relationship, as described in the previous paragraph, for whom a staff member becomes the main carer. An estimated six million people in the UK care for frail elderly, seriously ill or disabled people at home. When people become terminally ill, this need may continue for a matter of weeks or months, and a great deal of flexibility may be asked of the employer, from regular or irregular shorter or flexible hours to significant periods of extended leave, paid or unpaid.

The TUC and the Carers National Association produced a useful Charter for Carers in 1991.[6]

- Caring is difficult, demanding, and requires high levels of professional skills.
- Carers' own needs are important.
- Trade unions should oppose employment discrimination against carers and part-time workers.
- The TUC calls for adequately funded 'care in the community' without delay.
- The TUC calls for Government funding for support services for frail, elderly and disabled people, especially respite care. There should be sufficient provision to give all frail and disabled people a right to the support of professional carers.

- Trades unions should seek to negotiate flexible working packages from employers, including the same pay and benefits, pro-rata, as for other employees.
- Unions should press for a right for carers who have to give up work to return without loss of any employment rights.
- Training and retraining for carers and former carers returning to the labour market should be another union priority.
- Invalid Care Allowance should be extended to everyone who cares for another adult for 35 hours a week or more.
- The TUC calls for a statutory right to special leave.

An employer can help staff decide how to attend to the urgent and often distressing responsibility of ensuring that their nearest and dearest are adequately cared for when they can no longer look after themselves. It may include going part-time, working flexibly or giving up work for a period themselves. It may also mean that they need the employee's sensitive support, especially from their line manager, even if their working hours do not formally change.

Induction and Training

Great and expensive efforts are often made to recruit and select the right person for a job, only for it to be sabotaged by poor or even non-existent induction. It is an effective way of quickly demoralising and deskilling a potentially good recruit. This incompetence in induction is not always universal in a company. There may be careful induction for senior staff but none for others, or the other way round. Some managers may be casual, others rigorous. The Human Resources department may ensure induction happens, or it may not bother.

As part of induction, new staff need to be given information on what to do in the face of severe problems or a crisis at home that may impact on their work and what kind of support they might receive and from whom. They also need to be clear about family or compassionate leave policy, and to have a copy of this or easy access to one.

A large retailer trained all its welfare officers in counselling skills and active listening in relation to bereavement, so that they could conduct their meetings sensitively with the next-of-kin of staff or retired staff who had died, and also make good judgements about follow up and/or referral. Another prominent media company, without welfare staff, trained its Human Resource managers in the same way for the same reasons.

Thought also needs to be given to providing managers, supervisors and team leaders with:

- information and understanding of the bereavement process, and how it may affect staff;
- training in how to help affected staff and how to find further resources that they may be able to draw on, within and outside the company.

A Company Focal Point

Someone in the organisation needs to be identified as a focal point for good information about bereavement, which is likely to involve them in some introductory training in active listening, counselling skills and the bereavement process. That person needs to co-ordinate and monitor the work of any internal or external network of people offering staff support. Thirdly, they need to maintain up-to-date information, local and national, on support and training resources in this area of work. This book can form part of that.

In large organisations and those with scattered sites, there needs to be someone local with this role, supported and monitored by the person who acts as the company focal point.

These people can come from human resources or personnel, occupational health, welfare or line management. They do not need to occupy the role permanently, and the role can work well if it is passed on every two or three years – thus spreading the knowledge accumulated – so long as there is a good handover. In recruiting and selecting such a person, their experience outside work may be relevant. A line manager, for example, who is a volunteer youth counsellor in her spare time, may be a good person to take on this role, although in many cases it will fit comfortably into an established HR or welfare department.

Bereavement Counselling

People who can undertake bereavement support in-house should be identified, trained and briefed. A list of locally available external resources should also be compiled and publicised in the workplace. Bereavement counselling is described more fully in chapter 4, and Appendix 4 lists some relevant organisations in the field.

Those who have suffered a traumatic death and bereavement,

for example, as a survivor of a road traffic accident, are likely to need debriefing quickly. But bereavement counselling is not relevant in many cases, particularly in the early days, especially if people are well supported within the community. That community may include the workplace, as well as the extended family.

Some general practitioners, feeling no doubt under pressure themselves, apparently started to refer all their bereaved patients immediately to the local branch of the charity Cruse. The branch chair of counselling explained to them that bereavement counselling was often not needed by many of those who are bereaved, particularly in the early few weeks. It was more appropriate for those people who had had exceptionally difficult bereavements, were especially isolated or felt stuck after a period of time: counselling can help picking up on the unfinished business left over from community support.

As someone who has both received and provided bereavement counselling, I know how valuable it can be, but it must not be pushed excessively. To do so can undermine the confidence and will of colleagues, family and friends to provide the kind of support that is crucial to those of us when we are bereaved.

Notes

1. Moores, R. *Managing For High Performance*, (The Industrial Society, London, 1994).

2. O'Donoghue, John *Anam Cara: Spiritual Wisdom in the Celtic World* (Bantam Books, 1997).

3. Adams, Andrea *Bullying at Work* (Virago, London, 1992).

4. Ryan, Kathleen D. and Oestreich, Daniel K. *Driving Fear out of the Workplace* (Jossey-Bass, San Francisco, 1991).

5. *A TUC Guide, Family Leave*, (Trades Union Congress, London, 1994).

6. *A TUC Charter for Carers*, (Trades Union Congress, London, 1991).

3
How People at Work Can Help

- The Line Manager or Team Leader
- The Colleague
- Do's and Don'ts

In this chapter the roles of the line manager and colleague are summarised, and a short check list for the bereaved is included, as a guide for both of them. But first a short case study.

Martin talks about the support he received from his boss, after the diagnosis of his wife's advanced cancer:

> I used to think that my boss didn't manage people very well; but when the chips were down and I needed his help, he came through in a totally supportive human way that came as a real surprise. I felt that he could not have done it better.
>
> I was apprehensive yet clear when I went to tell him that I was going to resign from my full-time position, having invested ten years in what was a challenging and stressful job, latterly that of Business Group Manager. I explained that my wife's health had deteriorated and that I wanted and needed to spend more time with her and look after her as best I could. I also told him that I would be interested in approximately 4 or 5 days a month on a contract basis. I didn't say, but he undoubtedly guessed that this occasional work was important in maintaining our financial stability.
>
> As we talked, I felt his immediate sympathy and care. He said that he believed that I was making the right decision and that, at a time like this, family needs have to come first; furthermore he would do his best to ensure that I had as much work as I was able to undertake. It also helped when he told me that he knew that my leaving the full-time payroll would be a big loss to the organisa-tion. He followed this up by writing to my wife, telling her how much I would be missed and reassuring her that the company would support me to obtain part-time assignments so that she need not worry about our family finances.
>
> It has been two years since this conversation. I was able to be with my wife increasingly when she needed me and to spend some quality time with her when she was not feeling so ill, until she

passed away some months later. I continued to work on an occasional basis through this period and to make ends meet. Given the situation, we both helped each other and both derived some benefit as a result. It was a win-win conclusion, which resulted in building trust and respect, but it all started with his caring, flexible and imaginative response to my situation.

The Line Manager or Team Leader

1. Why take responsibility for supporting bereaved staff ?

(a) *Commitment to our people.* If we want the whole-hearted support of staff to their work and to the company, that commitment has to be reciprocal. We need to be committed to them as human beings, not as units of production or disembodied brains or 'hands' to be exploited without feeling. Bereavement is often an overwhelming experience and can and does happen to any of us. A manager committed to a staff member cannot ignore their needs at such a time, and will be concerned to provide appropriate support.

(b) *Commitment to the task and productivity.* Bereavement is a process that takes time, naturally and inevitably. It uses a great deal of emotional (and even physical) energy, some of which would otherwise be available for work. It is in our managerial interests that bereaved staff are supported through the process as well as possible, so that they are less likely to be alienated from their colleagues and the company and generally demotivated. The aim is to help them recover their ability to function positively in their life, including work, as soon as possible, without hurrying them artificially through the grieving process.

(c) *The whole-person approach.* Each of us has one brain in one body through which we live at work and away from work. We focus our energy and attention on the task in hand, at work or at home. But such mental boundaries are not to be confused with rigid barriers between our professional and personal lives. The whole person is always there. Coming through bereavement and work motivation are connected for most people.

2. Line managers, therefore, need to ensure that they know about a bereavement in order:

    (a) to communicate concern and support, both personally and on behalf of the company;

(b) to ensure that the company, including managers and colleagues, are behaving in a supportive and appropriate manner, and are encouraged and, if appropriate, helped to do so;

(c) to talk with the bereaved member of staff about their return to work and how they want to be supported after their return.

(d) to ensure that the individual is being as well supported as possible, being neither isolated nor swamped.

Be flexible about agreeing or even offering compassionate leave. In the case of terminal illness, such leave may be as important before a person dies as afterwards. It often makes for a better relationship with the employer if such leave is granted properly, rather than the bereaved staff member having to go for a sick note, although the general practitioner can be a valuable resource in helping some people work out when they are ready to go back to work.

In some cases this may involve the line manager providing direct support, but in others very little directly and personally, so long as the manager is satisfied that support is coming from other people. It will depend on:

- the needs and wishes of the bereaved staff member;
- counselling available in or through the company if required;
- the level of support being offered (and accepted) outside work;
- the interest and competence of the manager in this area.

3. Support should (given the above) be offered but not pushed.

Line managers at all levels who are involved in supporting staff in this way need themselves to have access to others on a confidential basis, so that they can consult about such matters as staff support and referral and/or off-load emotionally. The person thus consulted will need to find the right balance for both the bereaved member of staff and the manager by:

- supporting the manager to continue to provide support directly;
- giving some other help inside or outside the organisation;
- providing a judicious mixture of the two.

Others to whom managers might go is a matter of their choice. This might, for example, include their own senior manager and/or their personnel manager and/or others such as a colleague, trades union representative, an EAP (employee assistance programme), an internal or external counsellor or a specialist agency (such as CRUSE).

The Colleague

The survivor of a bereavement is 'catapulted', as Carol Staudacher has put it,[1] 'into a morass of responsibilities, requests for decisions, paperwork, and a stream of tedious, confusing, and often time-consuming details'. Some of this activity can be a way of occupying the mind so that the bereaved person is doing something practical in relation to their bereavement, while being distracted and protected temporarily from some of the painful feelings. Activity can help get the person through the worst of the early days. On the other hand, the pressure to do anything can also be incredibly hard for the person in the grip of acute grief (see chapter 6). Offers 'to pitch in', either by doing things or supporting the bereaved person to do things, can be a very real help. Examples could include any or all of the following:

- Make preliminary contact with a priest, minister, rabbi, the British Humanist Association or other spiritual representative.
- Make preliminary contact with a funeral director.
- Contact relatives and/or friends, who need to be notified.
- Contact the line manager or personnel/HR department and/or colleagues, and pass on instructions about what should be disseminated to others at work.
- Accompany him or her to register the death.
- Prepare and deliver a notice for the newspaper.
- Prepare and despatch invitations to the funeral, if appropriate.
- Help decide on flowers or donations (and if so, to what?)
- Provide and/or organise accommodation for visitors to the funeral coming from far away.
- Accompany the bereaved person to visit the hospital mortuary or the undertakers to view the body.

The following check list may be useful to discuss with someone who is bereaved or at least to guide your own support for them.

Do's and Don'ts

- Let yourself experience the pain of grief.
- Don't try to avoid the pain.
- Share how you feel with those(colleagues) with whom you feel safe.

- Don't be ashamed of your feelings – or your tears.
- Allow yourself more rest than usual: bereavement can be very tiring
- Don't fight the need to talk about it over & over again.
- Avoid heavy drinking (or illegal drugs) to dull the pain.
- Don't overdo work.
- Be cautious about major decisions in the early months.
- Don't take on new tasks or responsibilities too quickly.
- Expect the need to talk about your loss to continue for longer that you imagine.
- Don't be surprised if your concentration is affected.
- Break yourself in gently and gradually after a discussion with your manager.
- Don't be surprised if you have vivid and grief dreams.
- Try and be open about the kind of your support that you need (and don't need).
- Don't be ashamed of grief: it is part of loving and friendship.

Note

1. Staudacher, Carol *Men and Grief* (New Harbinger Publications, Oakland, CA, USA, 1991).

4

Bereavement Counselling

- What is Bereavement Counselling?
- Why Bereavement Counselling?
- How to Start?
- Timing

It has been estimated by Michael Reddy[1] that 80% of British companies use some form of workplace counselling. A particularly strong trend in recent years is that of Employee Assistance Programmes,[2] which give staff access to counsellors anonymously on a self-referral basis normally for a limited number of sessions, varying from 2 to 12.

There is a paradox about counselling. It is based on good, 'normal', human communication at its best, a process many of us undertake when we are functioning well. On the other hand, the experience of it can feel very different from the rest of our communications. This is because, for many of us, it is relatively rare to be on the receiving end of high quality, active listening, even though we benefit enormously from it. It can be simultaneously both ordinary and unusual, simple and highly skilled. Nowhere is this more evident than in dealing with death and bereavement.

What is Bereavement Counselling?

In many bereavements what counts most, and what is most needed, is quality support from friends, family and colleagues. If this is good enough, it will reflect consciously or unconsciously the skills of counselling, which underpin this book. But the word 'counselling' will probably never be used, nor need be. Where counselling differs from such support is not primarily in its content but its context.

- *Contract* – The counsellor is not only discreet, but will have an explicit contract of confidentiality and time which enhances the feeling of safety for the bereaved person (or client).

- *Independence* – The counsellor is normally outside the close circle of the client's acquaintances. The client is therefore likely to feel less responsibility for reassuring the counsellor that he or she is fine and coping well. There is often a great deal of subtle pressure on the bereaved to avoid sharing feelings honestly and thereby perhaps upsetting family, friends and colleagues, who may also be finding it difficult to cope. Although the sharing of grief can be crucially important for the future relationship of two people bereaved together, as for example with parents after the death of a child, the social pressure not to share deeply is frequently enormous.

- *Purpose* – The counsellor's task is to encourage the client to share the facts and the pain of the bereavement. The sole reason for the counsellor and client to meet is in order to facilitate this. In the counselling session there is no other distracting agenda to get in the way.

Why Bereavement Counselling?

There are a variety of reasons why such counselling can be especially helpful and these include:

Inability

The bereaved person does not feel able to express and work through his or her grief, due to its power and possibly the mistaken conditioning that to do so is self-indulgent, weak, counter-productive or a mixture of all three. (In such an instance, the person may become 'stuck' in one of the elements, for example, in depression or anger.)

Isolation

He or she is isolated from close, supportive relationships which may be characterised by taboos on sharing real feelings, with consequent embarrassment if the taboo is breached.

Trauma

The nature of the bereavement was itself especially traumatic; for example, in the death of a child or younger person; where dying has been particularly prolonged, painful or disfiguring; where it was felt to be avoidable; where it was especially sudden, as in an accident or an attack; or where it was cumulative. This last arises when several deaths come close together or at the same time, as in war, a major incident or disaster.

Because depth of feeling is such a subtle and varied component of a relationship, it is impossible to offer objective criteria: a subjective assessment is more realistic.

> Grace's boyfriend was killed in a plane crash on a business trip in the Far East. The wrong body was sent back and the real body was never found. Grace was a valued design engineer and her company were concerned to support her as well as they could. They arranged for some bereavement counselling. She felt that it helped her, not least to understand the powerful, grieving process through which she was going, and to keep her emotional bearings. What she found frightening was that for the first time that she could remember, her temper had got quite out of control on two occasions when there was no apparent link with her boyfriend's death. Her counsellor helped her acknowledge and express the anger in her grief, and understand the connections between her loss and her behaviour.

Work Pressure

If there are changes and other pressures and stresses at work already, a bereavement may stretch an individual's emotional resources too far. By putting back some much needed extra support, counselling may help to restore the emotional bank balance. In the case of Grace, her Personnel Director had two aims. One was to care for a person in a very vulnerable state, the other – more hard-nosed but as legitimate – was to maintain the level of her contribution to the company as far and as quickly as possible. It is hardly surprising that she had not been her 'old self' since the tragedy.

How to Start?

If external assistance may be helpful, the appropriate line or personnel manger should consult a counsellor or a suitable counselling organisation, such as those listed in Appendix 4, about the options open to the company. In doing so, it may be helpful to find out what code of ethics they subscribe to, such as that of the British Association for Counselling. The counsellor should agree a budget ceiling at the outset, although this may be delayed until after the first session, when the counsellor can better estimate with the client the length of time that may be needed. It can be helpful to work to a norm of between 4 and 10 sessions. Six is commonly used by a number of organisations. The norm may not be applied rigidly, but it underlines a sense that longer term counselling would not normally be funded by the employer. An exception to this would be if the bereavement or terminal condition has been clearly caused by or through work, irrespective of liability.

Alternatively the bereaved member of staff could be given information about options, such as help from a local branch of CRUSE, and supported to make the initial approach independently. But it is worth remembering that at such a time, it is often best if the ground work is done by another person. There can also be an advantage in having a small group of people in the company who have been trained in bereavement counselling or support. One of them can provide support to the staff member or his or her manager, and can perhaps help the bereaved person decide whether it is appropriate to seek further, external assistance.

Some organisations specialising in a particular cause of death, such as cot death, still birth, road traffic accidents and suicide, are among those listed in Appendix 4. They all bring their own kinds of questions, anxieties and pain. To lose someone close to you through such a cause can be bewildering and isolating, with a sense that you know so little about it, compared to the remote or inaccessible experts. For some people, to have access to sources of help and self help, information and mutual support can be extremely important.

Timing

Bereavement counselling, when it is appropriate, is often helpful after a few months or even a year or so, when immediate support is fading. The bereaved person may be going through a process of grieving, as described in the next two chapters, but start to find that there are issues which are still overwhelming or aspects of the bereavement that have not been addressed.

If the person finds that their return to some kind of normality at work and in other aspects of their life is painfully elusive, they may decide that counselling is worth trying. One person was referred by her Human Resources Director to a counsellor, for example, a year after losing her partner in an accident. Another young man referred himself to a counsellor 5 years after his bereavement when he finally admitted to himself that he was hopelessly stuck in trying to relate to members of the opposite sex as if they had to become a clone of his late wife. On the other hand, after a traumatic experience, counselling-based debriefing is likely to be desirable within a day or two. This is discussed further in chapter 8.

Notes

1. Reddy, M. (ed.) *EAPs and Counselling Provision in UK Organisations* (Independent Counselling and Advisory Service, Milton Keynes, 1993).

2. Feltham, Colin (ed.) *The Gains of Listening: Perspectives on Counselling at Work* (The Open University Press, Buckingham, 1997).

bereaved who, in usual contrast to himself, had an unusually thick growth of grey stubble because he'd been unable to face himself in the mirror since the death of his close partner. These aspects of 'self-neglect' can feel important as a message to others that there is a need for a response.

5

What are Loss and Bereavement?

- Defining Bereavement
- The Task of Bereavement
- Multiple Losses
- Secondary Losses
- The Impact of Bereavement on Relationships
- 'In Mourning'
- Bereavement: Public and Private

Defining Bereavement

Bereavement has been described as the process of adapting to loss incurred through death.[1] It involves grief, which often feels overwhelming in the case of someone important to you. Grief itself varies, according to a number of factors, such as the depth of the relationship and how timely the death may or may not have been. The dictionary[2] defines being bereaved as being bereft, which means to take away, especially by death. Bereavement can also mean that we have lost something or someone. It can feel either active or passive or both. We look further at efforts to make sense of this in chapters 11 and 16. The active and passive meanings of death also mirror our active and passive responses that are considered in chapter 6, Elements of Bereavement. Anger can stimulate a more active image of death as an enemy with whom we are drawn to struggle, while our sadness fits a more passive understanding of death, about which we can do nothing.

Although bereavement usually refers to a loss through death, the word is sometimes applied to other kinds of loss. From childhood we need to come to terms with various losses, such as toys, pets, leaving home to go to school, a change of school, moving home or a parent leaving home through a relationship split. We experience our parents' reaction to our distress, and also notice how they deal with their losses. This early conditioning contributes to our emerging personality and helps to prepare the ground for the way that we learn to cope with losses, including ultimately our own mortality.

The Task of Bereavement

Bereavement is a journey, in and through which we need to come to terms with the loss to the point where we can re-evaluate our life and move forward. This means beginning once more to value what we have, as well as what we have lost, so that we become slowly less preoccupied with what has gone. This is not to devalue the person who has died or what they meant to us, but is a matter of shifting the balance of attention towards what is still of value and makes our life worth living, even if at first this may be hard to find. The experience of bereavement involves a frequent and inevitable swing between the two processes of preoccupation with the loss and with the restoration of meaning in our present and future life: there is still something to live for after all.

William Worden has described four tasks of mourning:[3]

Task 1:   To accept the reality of the loss
Task 2:   To experience the pain or emotional aspects of the loss
Task 3:   To adjust to an environment in which the deceased is missing
Task 4:   To relocate the dead person within one's life and find ways to memorialise the person

The last is a response to the need to let go of the person, because there is also a deep sense that one will never, and indeed does not want to, forget a person who was important to one. Alice, aged 11, wrote down in her diary the day that her grandfather died: 'I will never forget Granddad.'

The task of bereavement is to begin to withdraw emotional energy from the relationship with the person who has died and to reinvest it in existing and new relationships with the living. Before we can do that, we must work through a series of powerful emotions, allowing as much time as is needed, which is often a great deal longer than is imagined. During this process, the bereaved person will swing between grief, during which they are experiencing and coming to terms with their loss, and restoration, when they are focusing on the present and learning to cope with the future without the deceased.

profound, changes in the way they live and think about their lives, especially if the person was close in practical as well as in emotional ways. The life together has itself died with the loss of the other person. A new life has to be created without them. There follows, therefore, a period of adjustment and, quite possibly, learning or even training, which is interwoven with the process of grieving. Cruse Bereavement Care has described this tension through a helpful model.

Experiences in Everyday Life

LOSS ORIENTED	>	RESOLUTION ORIENTED
Processing the loss	>	*Changes after loss*
Grief work	~	Doing new things
Intrusion of grief	~	Distraction from grief
Breaking bonds/ties	~	Denial/avoidance of grief
Denial/avoidance of	~	New roles/identities
Restoration/changes	~	New relationships

The bereavement process is seen as constantly moving back from being preoccupied with the loss to putting that on one side for the moment and getting on with life, but there is a tension in shifting our energy between two such demanding sets of needs. If one predominates, it can lead to repressing our grief and failing to allow it to begin to heal or, on the other hand, neglecting the basis of our life for the future: work, health and key relationships.

Such secondary losses may require resolute and enlightened compensatory changes in behaviour. New tasks may not fit gender stereotypes, which may have been part of the relationship previously. The elderly person, with a minimal overlap of roles in their past relationship, learns to live alone and to master new skills: cooking, paying the bills, changing a plug, doing the shopping, using the lawn mower or washing machine. A young husband with a job which takes him away a lot may have to find new, perhaps lower paid, work in order to be home for the children and manage a tighter budget. A young mother may have to find work outside the home or move to a smaller house in a different area if she cannot afford the mortgage. Children may have to change schools or no longer find anyone at home when they return from school.

So, as we have seen, the essence of bereavement is loss, even when apparently we are 'only' having to cope with a single death. We may through that death also be losing any combination of the following: companionship, support, a sexual relationship, parenting, help, knowledge, skills and experience shared with another person. A secondary loss is thus one which comes as a by-product of the main loss. Someone with whom we work closely dies and we find, for example, that we may have also lost:

- Someone who shares my enthusiasm for Bolton Wanderers;
- A tennis, fishing, drinking or bridge partner;
- Someone who could sort out the photocopier when it goes wrong;
- Someone else who could stand up to our boss, without him losing his temper;
- A person who knows what it is like to have worked for another company;
- A good sales person;
- Someone in the team who has a sense of humour compatible with mine;
- Someone at work who got on with my partner and helped to make social occasions at work enjoyable for her.

The Impact of Bereavement on Relationships

Fundamental to all good relationships is respecting and under-standing each other, a concept that is easy to write down, but much less easy to achieve. This acceptance can, however, often feel particularly difficult in the face of bereavement.

Marriages sometimes experience great pressure after bereave-ment due to the different ways of responding by the couple. After the death of a child, one person may feel the need to talk and the other, suffering from their own grief, find it hard to listen. One partner may avoid the subject, for fear of upsetting the other, who in turn meanwhile longs to talk. One spouse may be more private and the other more public with their feelings. In the private end of the spectrum, the person may keep their grief to themselves, talking a little to the other. The latter may want to talk and cry a lot with the other, not much on their own and also a great ideal with other people. One may seek some sexual comfort, consolation or even distraction, while the other is repelled by any thought of sex at such a time.

This kind of difference can also find expression in planning the funeral arrangements. One person may want to personalise the funeral with favourite music, personal tributes and reminiscences, while the other may find more comfort in formality or a traditional format, in which the expression of grief can be minimised and thus kept as private as possible. People are sometimes drawn to a partner, through the attraction of opposites, who is temperamentally very different to them. This can make it difficult in a bereavement for them to understand and meet each other's needs, particularly if both of them are exceptionally needy. Disappointment and even anger can build up, if it is not resolved through communication: at worst one person may feel disgust and contempt at the other's lack of restraint. 'It degrades the memory of our daughter.' On the other hand, the restraint of the other partner can be experienced as uncaring coldness.

In all good relationships there needs to be a balance between support and encouragement, on the one hand, and challenging or confronting, on the other. Support provides the foundations on which mutual understanding and respect is built, so that challenges can be experienced as acceptable and hopefully constructive, rather than feeling like an antagonistic attack. This applies to relationships at work as much as it does in the family or in other parts of our life.

The following model graphically depicts the impact on a partnership. Although it applies to partnerships in personal life, such as marriages and those between others with a long-term commitment to sharing their life with each other, it can also be related to strong working partnerships.

Stage 1: two people come together to develop an interdependent relationship. At an unconscious and a conscious level, people seem to be drawn to each other because of both their similarities and their differences. They may have striking physical facial similarities and shared values, beliefs or interests; but in personality and skills they may be very different. The result is that the partnership or team has a richness and strength that neither had as individuals, even though their differences may be a source of conflict needing to be sorted out to an extent at this stage. In the field of work, there are many public examples: Laurel and Hardy, Duke Ellington and Billy Strayhorn, Eric Morecambe and Ernie Wise, Frank Muir and Denis Nordern, Redgrave and Pinsent. They had different partners in their private life, but they worked together so well, because they complemented each other and became a team, a new unit. For this to work at its best, they moved towards:

Stage 2: they had got to know each other well enough, they had established a way of working or being with each other, so that they hardly had to think about it. Sometimes this understanding and knowledge were so powerful, they could predict each other's behaviour and thinking, so it almost becomes telepathic. The partners play to their strengths which can become exaggerated in the relationship. The opposite can also be true: each partner may become less confident, even deskilled, as they leave certain things to the other one. One of them dies and they are catapulted into:

Stage 3: they realise how they have come to depend on the other person, sometimes only feeling half-alive as a result themselves. At this point they may spasmodically look for an immediate replacement and prematurely try to recruit one, only to reject them because they never turn out to be the person they really want. There can be uncharacteristically promiscuous behaviour at this point, leading to some others feeling bitter and rejected. One way or another by going through the grieving process, they work towards:

Stage 4: they become something of a whole person again, though different from where they were on their life journey, when they were at Stage 1. At this point, they will be far readier (than in Stage 3) to move into a new relationship, in which their new partner will not be in such danger of forever being compared unfavourably with the, possibly idealised, deceased one.

Stephen and John had been together for nearly 10 years, and those who knew them thought of them as a great team, partly because they complemented each other so well. The sum was definitely greater than the parts! Within their relationship, however, those differences that were such a strength on good days were on bad days a source of conflict and tension, when they found it hard to accept each other.

Nevertheless, after John's death in a road traffic accident, Stephen found himself grieving as much for the creative spontaneity and even chaos as for the order in their relationship. The secondary losses he experience included John's gift for fresh ideas, for reaching out to people and dealing assertively with the difficult ones. Without the reality of the day-to-day irritations in their relationship, he was able to see more clearly what a great team they were. He often asked himself why it should have taken John's death for him to get in touch with that realisation again.

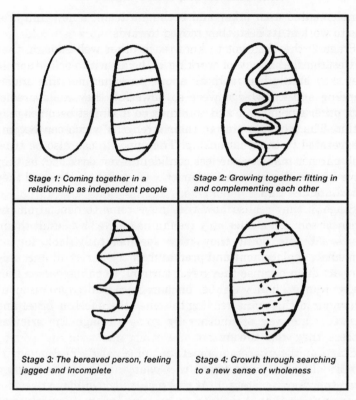

Stage 1: Coming together in a relationship as independent people

Stage 2: Growing together: fitting in and complementing each other

Stage 3: The bereaved person, feeling jagged and incomplete

Stage 4: Growth through searching to a new sense of wholeness

'In Mourning'

Many people will experience bereavement without necessarily feeling the intensity of feelings often described in this book. The terms 'bereavement', 'grief' and 'mourning' are sometimes used almost interchangeably to describe our reaction to death. 'Grief' is a strong word for sorrow in the face of a major loss, whereas 'mourning' has two meanings: grieving itself or a period of time, given over to grieving. The clothes worn to show grief when someone dies are an aspect of the latter, although that custom has diminished in the past generation or two.

On a personal basis, someone may be thought of as 'in mourning' for very variable periods: the time in which they are, or at least allow others to see that they are, preoccupied by their loss. Society also prescribes periods of mourning. In some cultures this may be a month, in others a few days. In England for many there is a convention that it lasts from the death to the funeral, after which the bereaved are expected to become more self sufficient again and 'back to normal', as if they have used up their quota of sympathy. At its best, this norm gives permission to grieve openly and also a steer to move forward. The consequence of this subtle pressure is that people make great efforts to hide what may be reservoirs of grief from others as a social duty. It is as if a sign is required that they are strong enough to look after themselves and are free from the excesses of self indulgence, which is the cruel veneer that is sometimes expected from the bereaved, not least in the workplace that is more dysfunctional in human terms.

It is not a new phenomenon. In the Bible, the author of chapter 53, verse 3, of the Book of Isaiah writes of 'a man of sorrows, and acquainted with grief' or 'humbled by suffering', in the New English Bible translation: 'and we hid as it were our faces from him; he was despised, and we esteemed him not'. In this we have an echo of the modern message to those who are in mourning that, if they want to be popular, they need to get out of mourning fairly smartly. To praise a bereaved person for coping so well can sometimes deliver the same message. The subtext reads: coping well means not upsetting, depressing or embarrassing the rest of us by showing too much grief. Books such as this are hopefully encouraging a change in our the culture towards a more understanding and accepting attitude to those 'in mourning', so that they have to pretend less to those close to them at work or at home about how they are really feeling.

Bereavement: Public and Private

Bereavement is experienced individually and sometimes collectively. The isolation and loneliness felt can be particularly hard if you feel that nobody else cares deeply about the death of someone to whom you are very close. Nevertheless, as we are social animals, so in various ways and to various degrees grief can be shared – within a work team, a family or some other small or large circle of people. Its pain may have significance for us as a species, serving the function of binding the social group, the group that is essential for our survival. We have a sense of what we value, and therefore need to look after with special care, partly though the intensity of our grief. As a society we normally see the death of a child or young person as more tragic than that of an older person or a well-loved pet.

Public outpourings for the premature and violent deaths in our own century have been many: Gandhi, Steve Biko, President Kennedy and his brother Robert, Martin Luther King and even John Lennon. A dramatic recent example of collective grieving was the public response to the sudden death in a Paris car crash on 31 August 1997 of Diana, Princess of Wales. After a week of people queuing to get into our town centre church in Rugby to sign the Book of Remembrance and make donations to her charity, I was taking a service in the same church the following Sunday. Several people were crying as they took their communion, and I spoke to one young woman who stayed behind too upset to move. I asked her if her tears were about Diana. 'They are partly', she replied 'but they are mainly for my father who died four months ago and I haven't realised how much I missed him till this week'. She explained further that it had struck her forcibly how it felt to her that, although she greatly loved her father, his death had not been properly acknowledged when it happened. In stark contrast, for Diana the crowds had gathered as the media chose her death to dominate their space.

The whole experience paralleled publicly the way grief can totally preoccupy us as individuals, at least initially. This outpouring of feelings brought home to many that if we really care about someone, they may also warrant, at least in their own circle of family and friends, the level of mourning that was focused on Diana nationally and even internationally. For many her death felt a very personal loss, but for others there was a sense of her as a symbol of much that was good and beautiful, combined with the special tragedy of an avoidable and violent death to someone still young.

Collective grieving also occurs in response to disasters, in which many people die, such as happened at Hillsborough or to the Herald of Free Enterprise. Colin and Wendy Parry have written a powerful book, which highlights the amazing public response, which was by no means restricted to their home town, to the terrible murder of their son Tim and of young Johnathan Ball by the IRA in the Warrington bombing[4] on 20 March 1993, also in England. The bombs that killed and injured so many at the East African US embassies in Nairobi and Dar es Salaam or in Omagh, Northern Ireland in 1998 all induced massive experiences of public grieving, uniting people in a strong sense of their common humanity.

When the media and members of the public, who did not know

the people who have died, become involved in a bereavement, it is as if they unofficially represent the community. At worst such attention can be intrusive and make the tragedy harder to bear; at best a real comfort. The latter is perhaps particularly relevant with acts of terrorism, where suffering and deaths are caused deliberately by other inhuman beings.

The public response is not only a way of sharing, albeit perhaps only in a small way, the grief of the immediately bereaved, but also a way of disassociating themselves from the atrocity to reinforce the message that it is only a tiny minority of monsters engaged in such behaviour. The whole world has not gone mad. Such a crumb of comfort is not available to the victims of ethnic cleansing, where the majority appear to turn on a minority, whether in Nazi Germany or the more recent examples of Pol Pot's Cambodia, the Kurds, Rwanda, Kosovo or East Timor.

This role of representing the wider community can be fulfilled in a more discreet way by the work organisation, along with any other organisations associated with the person who has died, such as sports, arts or a voluntary, religious or political group. Ways in which the organisation can express such support have been already discussed in chapter 2, How the Organisation Can Help.

At its root bereavement is an intensely personal experience, even when it is shared. That sharing can be a mixture of shared grief and support from others, who are grieving less strongly themselves but who have a commitment to those mainly suffering the loss. The closer the bereaved person is to the one who has died, usually the more painful the loss is. It seems to be an unavoidable equation. The deeper the friendship or love we feel for each other, potentially the deeper is the pain and the longer is the process of mourning. But there is a paradox too: while on one level death changes everything in a relationship, on another level the experience of loss can often seem to change nothing of the feelings towards the person who has died. Edith Sitwell (1957) in some famous lines put this as follows:

> Love is not changed by Death
> and nothing is lost
> and all in the end is Harvest.[6]

The news that Jean had been killed the previous day in a gliding accident traumatised the whole working group in the open plan office for a long time. She'd been young, healthy and full of life. An empty desk, normally such a mundane phenomenon, became a focal point of disbelief and sadness. For a time it was left empty as her personal belongings were removed. Eventually, her successor was appointed to the uncomfortable task of stepping into 'dead woman's shoes', and making Jean's work space her own.

Jean had been popular when alive, but her popularity became exaggerated in death, as the irritating aspects of her behaviour were mostly forgotten out of respect for her memory. After all, her colleagues were now free of those negative aspects of her; so consequently she became a harder act to follow than if she had lived and moved to another job.

In departmental gossip, her successor, Annabel, tended to be compared unfavourably with Jean, although a couple of people stuck up for her and went out of their way to make her feel welcome. They were the main ones to have quarrelled with Jean frequently and wanted to ensure that the guilt they felt after her death was in no danger of being repeated a second time. In any case they personally found Annabel a good deal easier to get along with.

All of the above could have applied if Jean had not died but had left her job anyway. She might, for example, have taken off for a new life in another place, have got a better job, been fired or made redundant. The suddenness of such an accident can be similar in the last two examples. Extremely unenlightened employers can get people out of the building immediately after informing them that their job has been made redundant and that there are no alternative employment possibilities for them within the company. The staff member may have been trusted until that moment, but be immediately regarded as a potential saboteur and thief, once redundancy strikes.

The beginning of motivating those who remain is influenced by how those who go are treated. It can be a great mistake to fail to offer the latter time to process the ending of their job and farewells in the company. They usually need and want some opportunity, with reasonable support from colleagues and others, to collect their thoughts and feelings and begin to move towards the next chapter of their working lives. With dismissal for misconduct, the norm would be to leave at once because staff members have already shown themselves to be unreliable and possibility dishonest. Guilt about them is often minimised because they are thought, in part at least, to have brought their fate upon themselves. Good managers will feel some guilt or at least an element of personal responsibility in most dismissals on the grounds of misconduct or incompetence, because there is usually some leadership failure in the areas of selection, induction, training, motivation or supervision.

Even though the feelings of anguish can be powerful in any of these situations of sudden separation, where a working group is disrupted, separation through death, however, usually produces a response in others that is a great deal stronger than in other situations. Its finality and immediacy are so powerful. The death of someone who has already left the work group, for example, to go to another job or to retire, is less immediate. In such cases, the work group is likely to have reformed. The grieving on an individual level may be just as strong, but less so collectively. Colleagues may miss the grieving, consequently, because it is more private and probably somewhat concealed. The death of a colleague, recently retired, may be a source of acute sadness to those with whom a close relationship had been built. The group as a whole, however, may be relatively unaffected, in a way that would not have applied if the person had died while still in harness.

Notes

1. Worden, W. *Children and Grief*, (Guildford Press, New York and London, 1996).

2. *New Generation Dictionary*, (Longman, London, 1981).

3. Worden, W. *Grief Counselling and Grief Therapy*, (Tavistock, London, 1983)

4. *'Life Change Index' From Strategies in Self-Awareness*, The Marylebone Health Centre, 17 Marylebone Road, London NW1 5LT, UK Stroebe & Schut, (1995).

5. Parry, Colin & Wendy, *Tim: An Ordinary Boy* (Hodder and Stoughton, 1994)

6. Bowlby, J. *Attachment and Loss: Loss, Sadness and Depression* (Basic Books, New York, 1980).

6

Elements of Bereavement

- Introduction
- Three Phases of Grief
- Relief
- Parallels in the Bereavement Process and Preparation for Death
- The Process of Loss

Introduction

The focus of this chapter is on the kind of grieving process that people tend to go through. It is not a map marking the exact route, because bereavement is such an individual experience that it is foolish to imagine we can describe with any precision the journey beforehand. Colin Parry, for example, wrote[1] after the murder of his son, Tim, by the IRA in Warrington that he and his wife Wendy 'learned that people do not grieve according to schedules and timetables. There are wild and irrational mood swings. There were times when grief and anger overcame me and she appeared calm and controlled. There were times when the raw emotion was hers, and I was numb and frozen'.

The more the process of bereavement is understood, the more the feelings experienced can seem highly rational. On closer examination, it becomes apparent that they follow a logic of their own, even though they often seem unpredictable. Furthermore, the process is not switched off, like a gas fire, when the person touched by death comes to work, however hard he or she may try to control their feelings. If the person was feeling overwhelmed yesterday, it does not mean that they will be today. Bereavement has been described as an emotional switchback, difficult to follow, especially in someone else, which is why it is so important to respect the person, however they are feeling, if you are trying to support them. Support requires, therefore, noticing and accepting how the person is at any particular moment.

For some people, to be able to share what they are going through from time to time with others at work may be really helpful. At times this may even be necessary for them to feel that they can get through a working day. For others their grieving may be more private or at least shared with family or friends away from the workplace.

Three Phases of Grief

Below, the process of loss is described in more detail, but sometimes it is easier to simplify its essence. One example is to identify three main aspects:

Denial	which can include shock, disbelief, fantasy and numbness;
Pain	which may include experiencing grief through, for example, anger, depression, apathy, guilt, searching, pining and feelings of worthlessness;
Acceptance	adjusting to life without the person who has died and becoming ready to engage in new activities and relationships, relocating energy from the past into the future.

This movement from stage to stage and back again is characteristically an unconscious process. Consequently the bereaved person does not usually feel as if they are in control of their mood changes, which are often so painful that we would be unlikely to choose consciously to enter them. It can feel as if it is happening to us, outside our control, but is a process necessary for recovering the possibility of happiness. Mood swings are a normal, perhaps barely noticed, part of human experience. What makes them remarkable in bereavement is their power. When the swing happens, it can feel like a setback. It is, however, just as likely to be a step forward as conscious awareness of our feelings recurs and we experience and maybe express some more of the distress from our loss.

To describe the elements of bereavement can be both useful but also misleading. They can be put in an apparently logical sequence, but the reality is usually different. People move from one to another and then loop back to an earlier stage. Healing comes for many as the feelings come to the surface and begin to dissipate bit by bit. We may step backwards in order to deal with pain at a deeper level than before, now that we are ready for it.

We may however, also be propelled out of a stage, if only temporarily, because of the need for a break from its intensity and to get on with the rest of our life.

The different sections in this chapter can, therefore, be seen as some of the landmarks people may go past or through, though not necessarily in the order they appear in the model we are using here. The order approximates the route quite a few people follow. It cannot be stated too strongly that the journey may vary from that in the model for many people. It may happen in any or all of the following four ways:

- The order may be different from that of the model;
- Going back to some elements repeatedly is common;
- Some of the elements may be apparently missed out altogether or passed over so lightly that they appear insignificant by comparison with the others;
- Aspects of the process may be delayed for some people, until triggered by later events.

Relief

Bereavement is not always completely unpleasant. The power of the good memories and the sense that the quality of life that has been shared with the person who has died can make the experience sweet as well as bitter. Comfort can also be drawn from the way others express their love and admiration for the person who has died. One widow told me; 'I knew how much I loved him but I had no idea until he died how many people he worked with thought so much of him too'. The irony is that the deceased person may not have realised it either. Even allowing for an element of rose-tinted sentimentality, it sometimes takes someone's death for us to realise how much we valued him or her.

An element of relief can also ameliorate the worst part of bereavement. The quality of life may have deteriorated to the point where death seemed to be the lesser of two evils or even the 'blessed relief' of stereotyped Victorian religion, devoted as it was so often to looking forward to a life after death. Alternatively, where the relationship was acrimonious, there may be a sense of liberation from an undue element of conflict, quarrelling or nagging. Where the relationship felt claustrophobic, the freedom to choose to do what you want, rather then always being expected to fit into the incessant demands and preferences of a boss, colleague or partner, can be tremendous.

The relief can be very real even in what might be for some a trivial matter. One widow told me after the death of her husband that she liked the fact that she could choose what to watch on television. This does not necessarily make the process easier. The relief can be complicated by guilt and by regret for what was missing from the relationship. The finality of death creates an inability to ever improve it. There can be an element of grieving for the unfulfilled hopes for the relationship that never was.

Most relationships, good ones as well as bad, are characterised by ambivalence or mixed feelings towards each other. These are usually present at some level, even if unconscious, and are arguably healthy and necessary if our partner is a fallible, real human being. Additionally, people in relationships need space as well as closeness. At work, we may have had hopes and fantasies that a colleague or boss would be the perfect one, but getting to know them as real people involved the halo slipping.

Parallels in the Bereavement Process and Preparation for Death

The process of bereavement overlaps with the stages of the emotional response to dying described in chapter 12, Preparing for Dying and Death. This is sometimes noticed, perhaps in retrospect, by a bereaved person who has supported someone in their journey towards death. Indeed the sharing of that sorrow can be a source of comfort to both the dying person and the one to be left behind and can give them both the sense that their love for each other on one level is stronger than death. For the survivor, however, the helplessness in their anticipatory grief can be agonising, as they come to realise that they are powerless to prevent the death of someone for whom they care so deeply.

Am I Going Mad?

Because the feelings can be so strong and unfamiliar, people grieving deeply, especially for the first time, not infrequently feel that they are going mad. This can be reinforced through some of the dreams and nightmares that the bereaved experience.

While asleep, the mind continues to work through the bereavement process. Just as some of the feelings are unfamiliar and often extremely powerful when we are awake, so dreaming allows the mind to range free from the constraints of logic or consciousness into the further recesses of grief. An example came from Andrea, a young school teacher, who told me about a dream that she had after the death of her grandfather, to whom she had been very close:

> We were sitting around in the cottage, in the sitting room. Granddad couldn't speak or move because he was dead, and just sat there. Everyone else carried on as if he wasn't there. I was sitting opposite him, and I could communicate with him. I was the only one who could hear him. I told him I loved him. It felt as if it was just the two of us, so close – and that no one else mattered.

The person who successfully repressed the feelings of bereavement the first time it happened to them may experience a double dose the second time round. This may be particularly significant for bereaved adults, who have previously suffered a major loss as a child. It is discussed further in chapter 9, Children and Young People.

To learn from a colleague or friend that these feelings are normal can be reassuring: it will not protect the individual from the power of the pain, but it helps to know that others have walked that road and perhaps understand a little. It is also highly likely that they are not going 'mad', but rather experiencing a very powerful aspect of grief, which will in time most likely pass or become less overwhelming.

Bereavement and Time Scales

Acute grief is part of the ongoing task of mourning and can continue for months, sometimes years. Some people start to feel guilty even after a week if they have not 'got over it' and even more so if their acute grieving is still going on after a month. It is better to anticipate the possibility of months spent in this phase, on and off: two years is not unusual, although it is impossible to generalise. It means that work concentration and motivation may continue to be affected, perhaps only intermittently. Allowance should be made for that. With a valued member of staff, this approach will be a good investment in terms of their longer term contribution and morale.

> Margaret's mother died on Thursday. The following Monday, she was greeted at work by a friend and colleague with a crisp smile and an equally bright, 'All right, then?'

Supporting people in bereavement is unlikely to be like a 100 metres sprint. For the bereaved person it is more likely to feel like a marathon with the finishing line ever receding from view, however hard they try. The bereaved frequently experience guilt or anxiety because they cannot pull themselves together and 'snap out of it'. They feel or are made to feel that they are boring and poor company, because of their continuing preoccupation with their loss. They may need to share repeatedly the story of what happened and to go over again and again what especially hurts. This involves talking, but also discharging feelings by crying, laughing and raging, sometimes one after the other, sometime together. That may need a colleague or friend or two with the commitment, patience and understanding of why this is important, and the listening skills to let them get on with it.

Every time the bereaved person goes through how their loved one died, or the row they had recently or the wonderful times they had together or whatever else may be particularly difficult, they are likely to be peeling off another layer of the pain. Although it may seem like repetition, it is never quite the same the second, third, fourth or fifth time. To understand that progress in healing comes through apparent repetition is crucial in supporting the bereaved. An experience of such magnitude often needs and demands quantity as well as quality of support. Although much of it will be resolved away from work, recovery from bereavement is not an area in which to expect quick results. It is a half-marathon, not a sprint.

Compassion fatigue can easily affect those who initially offer more than they are able to sustain. They may feel the need to withdraw. This can mirror the desire of most bereaved people at work to focus on getting to grips with their job as soon as possible. This should not, however, be confused with the idea that they have necessarily 'got over it'. Long-term working relationships require an equally long-term balance between concentrating on the job and commitment to the well-being of the person.

The Process of Loss

1. Shock	– Numbness, protection from emotions, which might otherwise be overwhelming.
2. Acute Grief	– Raw, overwhelming sadness: compulsion to think about the loss despite pain.
	– High arousal – the fight or flight response.

3. Defence Mechanisms

a. Denial — An optimism that may feel unreal:
'it is a release from their suffering so there is no need to be sad for them.'
'the person has gone to a better place, so I must be happy for them.'
'maybe the person did not die after all.'

b. Searching — Occasionally a physical search for dead person; revisiting places associated with them.

c. Avoidance — Hyperactivity: too busy to allow painful feelings to surface.

d. Pretence and Fantasy — Behaving as though loss has not occurred:
— Prince Albert's shaving water continued to be put out daily after his death.

e. Bargaining — Often with God, regardless of faith: 'bring him back and I promise I will ….'

4. Fear — Of violent emotions; of going mad; of an inability to cope.
— Often worse at night; vivid dreams and nightmares.

5. Guilt — 'If I had/hadn't done X … this would never have happened.'
— 'I was so bad that this happened'.

6. Anger and Resentment — With self, dead person, doctors, God, the boss, the company, heartless colleagues etc.
— 'Why me?'
— Often misdirected onto those close to the bereaved.
— Feels inappropriate.

7. Depression — Emotional exhaustion.

8. Loneliness — Withdrawal, apathy, lowering of standards, regression.

9. Resolution — Resignation/acceptance.
— Emotional energy withdrawn from the lost person, job, home etc. and reinvested into the present and the future.

10. Introjection — Internalising the qualities of the person who has died.

1. Shock

Even when death is expected, its arrival usually comes as a shock, lasting from a few minutes to a few days. The function of shock is to enable us to carry on somehow for a limited time. It protects us from the full impact of what has happened, whether we have lost a limb in an accident or an emotional limb through the death of someone close to us.

Shock can be expressed in panic, numbness or a mixture of the two. The first leads to the hyperactivity that is well-suited to dealing with the practical arrangements associated with the aftermath of death, such as informing people, arrangements with funeral directors and the funeral itself. The second is the complete opposite: an apathy, which requires everyone else to do everything, including if possible looking after the bereaved person.

Dick's mother phoned him at 6.30 a.m. to tell him that his father had just died from a heart attack. By 8.30 a.m. he was on his way to the other side of the country where his parents lived. He had already written a two page email to his secretary and put through a coherent ten minute phone call to his deputy unscrambling his plans and ensuring that essential work was undertaken in his absence. He was able to be relatively competent because his state of shock shielded him for the moment from the reality and emotional impact of what had happened.

He did not feel anything very much, except for the adrenaline surge to get cracking fast. On one level, he did not really believe it had happened. He was conscious that he wanted to see his father's body to be sure. The shock acted like a protective blanket to prevent him being overwhelmed and incapacitated.

2. Acute Grief

Shock is usually penetrated, sometimes within minutes, by sharp, sudden waves of acute grief in which the bereaved person is in a state of high arousal and agitation. It is characterised by the 'fight and flight' response, which is also found in fear, anger and physical pain. This is a phase when the ability to function well at work, school or home is diminished to the point of being non-existent. The person is completely absorbed in what has happened, as it begins to spear its way through the protective blanket of shock to reveal intense yearning and longing. It has been described as feeling as if the dead person has been torn out of your body. It can be accompanied by a variety of physical symptoms, such as feeling cold and clammy, an increased heart-rate, anorexia, nausea, 'butterflies' in the stomach, frequently passing urine, diarrhoea and insomnia.

Moments as intense as this can recur many years after the person has died.

Although thinking about the death is acutely painful, the need to do so is compulsive, despite the pain. It is a time of raw sadness, of restlessness and often sleeplessness, and of the need to talk, reflect, rage and weep. When asleep or just waking, hallucinations and strange vivid dreams are common. Acute grief can be very upsetting to be near, and so can stimulate a desire to avoid someone in acute grief.

Elizabeth Jennings (1967) wrote of this phase:

> Time does not heal.
> It makes a half-stitched scar
> That can be broken and you feel
> Grief as total as in its first hour.

What typically changes is not its intensity but its continuity. At first the bereaved person may be constantly moving in and out of it, but as the days or weeks pass, longer intervals will gradually elapse between being preoccupied with and pining for the deceased. But its power may feel as great when it does return. It is 'the heartbreak in the heart of things', as W.W. Gibson wrote, the potential price of any genuine friendship and love.

When the baby of a colleague died in tragic circumstances, Joan's own work suffered. When her manager talked through what was troubling her, falteringly she told him that she had lost a baby at the same age, 5 years before. She was particularly troubled because the incident had brought memories flooding back. A painful aspect of that had been her GP telling her that she was grieving 'abnormally', because she was still so upset six months after the event. It was as if he had twisted a knife in the wound of her grief and added a further unnecessary burden of stress.

That word 'abnormal' had stuck in her throat ever since. She was torn between her anger at the offensive insensitivity of the GP and her sneaking suspicion that the doctor may have been right and she was 'abnormal' as well as desolate at the loss of the child she loved so intensely.

3. Defence Mechanisms

a. Denial

The value of denial in bereavement is that it helps protect us from the necessity of coming to terms with all the pain at once. To register the reality of death at a deep level seems to involve the need to question the fact of it in a variety of ways. Few people actually literally deny the death, although it is more likely to occur in rare cases where the body has not been found or at least seen by the bereaved person. Perhaps a mistake was made and s/he is not really dead:

> 'I just can't believe that he really has gone.'
> 'I keep thinking that he is going to walk through that door this evening just like he always has.'
> 'I feel as if I'm going to wake up and find out that it was a bad dream after all.'

Denial can be reflected in vivid dreams, in which the dead person is alive again, or sometimes in waking dreams, in which the person's presence is felt, usually but not always invisibly.

A person may be helped to come to terms with the reality of death by seeing and spending time with the body, either at the undertaker's chapel of rest or hospital or by keeping the body at home until the funeral. When my father died, his body stayed at home so that members of the family could say their farewells in their own time, at their own pace. In war, accidents or disasters, it may not be possible to see the body and can in consequence be more difficult to accept that the person has really died.

On the other hand, this does not apply universally, and some wish that they had not seen the person after death, especially if the body has been laid out badly, with for example the mouth dropping open. A dead body soon looks and smells unlike the person who has died, even quite recently. So, those who have not seen the body of their loved one after death do not need to feel that they have missed something essential, as the arguments on this issue are often finely balanced.

Of course it is often not a matter of choice, for example, for the person who finds someone dead or is required by the police to identify a body of a person close to them.

A variation on the theme of denial is the acceptance of the fact of death but a refusal to acknowledge the pain of bereavement, sometimes on the basis of religious belief.

> The mother of Liam and Beryl told them that they must not be sad about their young son, because he had passed on to be with Jesus. This piety felt so false to the mourning parents that it helped to break their links with the church for about 10 years.

At work, the bereaved person's use of denial in thinking and talking realistically only some of the time with only some people needs to be respected. Equally, it is not helpful to impose denial on the person because of everyone else's discomfort with what has happened. Striking the right balance requires awareness and sensitivity.

Denial can also be expressed through humour and behaviour that appears to take no account or inadequate account of the person's death. It is a coping mechanism used by some in professions where death or dead bodies are familiar experiences.

> Rick, one of the computer programmers, committed suicide by hanging himself: he had a young family and money troubles. He had kept himself to himself, so his colleagues did not know him too well. The response of the majority was to express no sympathy but to 'slag him off' as weak and stupid. One of his colleagues felt very differently, however, as his own brother had died in the same way two years before. He found it hard to come to terms with the lack of compassion in the others for the desperation Rick had presumably felt before he took such a step.

b. Searching

Searching, like most of the so-called stages, can be a layer of the bereavement process, which takes many different forms. Sometimes it takes the form of a physical search, such as visiting old haunts or the hospital or place where the death occurred, hoping in some strange way to find the deceased person there. A preoccupation with places, objects or memories associated with the person who has died, such as photographs, letters and possessions is characteristic of searching. Contact with old friends or family may all play their part in a kind of modern pilgrimage. Our efforts to rediscover in some way the person we have lost can also have a religious dimension.

Many newly bereaved seek out spiritualist churches or visits mediums in the hope of making contact with the deceased. An interest in a life after or beyond death need not, however, be dismissed as merely wishful thinking for victims of superstitious suggestibility. At such a time, we may be in a state of heightened sensitivity to dimensions of spiritual reality. It is also possible that there may be a bit of both.

The search for all the fragmented memories of the dead person helps to internalise them, so that they can be remembered in the inner world of the mind now that they no longer exist 'out there' and no longer exist only as an absence in the outer world. In the ancient myth of Isis, she searches the universe for all the dismembered parts of Osiris in order to remember him. Part of the search is to restore the other in memory, which can fade quickly especially with someone with whom we have been very close.

In doing this, the bereaved may also be reconstructing themselves with a new identity or recovering their old one, and remaking their understanding of the world in which such an event has happened. Work can be a sheet anchor, even a sign of hope, which is why a redundancy and a bereavement coming together can feel so catastrophic. 'It seemed like the end of the world'. It was the end of the previous world of meaning.

c. Avoidance

A common defence mechanism is to avoid thinking or talking about the loss. An effective way of achieving this is to become hyperactive, too busy to allow painful feelings to surface. One becomes preoccupied with other activities either on quite a mundane level, such as maintaining home, garden and work, moving house, or by taking on demanding new activities. They can insist on organising the funeral single-handed and disposing of the deceased's belongings immediately, possibly to regret doing so later.

It can lead people rushing back to work too soon, before they are really ready, and taking on new projects unnecessarily. The former can help counter the destabilising impact of grief, which means that extra care and concentration are required to be competent in everyday living, most especially activities that are potentially dangerous, such as driving.

At work it is important at least to consider whether a newly bereaved person can be given a break from such activities. In the shorter term, support and supervision may need to be stepped up. Whether this is done discreetly or openly will depend on the personalities and relationship with the bereaved person. They may need to be given shorter runs and encouraged to take things slowly and carefully, for the sake of others as well as themselves.

d. Pretence and Fantasy

Denial is sometimes extended to the point of pretending that the person is not really dead. It can take many forms such as talking aloud with the person, as if he was alive, and maintaining his things in place, maybe even putting out clean clothes or laying a place at table for him. Queen Victoria ordered Prince Albert's shaving water to be put out daily after his death. Such pretence can play a useful, if intermittent, role in helping someone cope. Occasionally it becomes more prolonged and then, as with other defence mechanisms, may block the grieving process if the person becomes stuck in this phase.

The accidental laying of an extra place at the meal-table or other routines do not constitute pretence: they may just be forgetfulness. Imaginary conversations with the dead person can be also held in full awareness of the fact that he or she has died, and be a source of great comfort. Conversing with someone who has died can be a way of letting the relationship go more gradually and gently than the suddenness of death permits. It can also express a belief, conviction or hope that the person is in spirit not only still alive but also able to hear human words directed towards them. Behaviour tends to change at a slower pace than changes in our understanding or attitude. It is hardly surprising that those who do not believe that the deceased still exists in some way continue to behave as if the person was still alive, even though they may think intellectually that this is not so.

e. Bargaining

A final example of a common defence mechanism is bargaining, which often has a deep psychological power, even if rationally we believe that nothing can be achieved. We may be drawn to try trading good behaviour, extra effort, prayer or personal sacrifice in the hope that the person may be contacted again, perhaps the death was all a big mistake or, if it was not, then there may at least be contact with them beyond the grave.

4. Fear

C.S. Lewis opened his short book about the death of his wife, *A Grief Observed*, 'No-one ever told me how like fear grief is'.[2] There are many different fears associated with some bereavements, although few individuals are likely to experience them all. These include the fear of unfamiliar strong emotions, of going mad, of being alone in the house, of not surviving practically and/or emotionally without the deceased, of other people dying next or of following the deceased into illness and/or into death.

Especially for those who have not been bereaved before, the experience can be frightening partly because it is so unfamiliar. Even if the bereaved do not feel that they are going mad, they can seem like strangers to themselves, reacting in a way that has not been experienced before. Their usual sense of identity may feel lost or out of control as they are swept along by complex, swiftly changing and often violent emotions. Their bond with the dead person can make them feel strange or alienated from other people. If this is reinforced by others actually withdrawing from them, the nightmare can intensify.

The nightmare can be literal, and it is sometimes helpful to ask the bereaved if they are having particularly vivid or strange dreams. The dream sometimes involves the death or the deceased person coming back to life or living in another place.

Mary dreamt that her mother had phoned to say she was living in a town 20 miles away, and wanted to see her new grandson. It stirred up some confusing and painful feelings for her, as her mother had died when she was a young child. Although she was now in her mid 20s and happy with her partner, when Mary had become pregnant and her baby was born, she had missed her mother greatly. Her unconscious mind had brought out thoughts that she had no idea were lurking there. Supposing her mother had not died and was living elsewhere and was getting in touch? How wonderful, but then how could she have neglected Annabel all these years?

The dream brought out her feelings of betrayal by her mother for dying, even though her rational mind knew that she could not be blamed for her terminal illness. At a conscious level there was no room for her anxiety or anger. Dreams can play a powerful, fascinating and useful role in linking our unconscious to our conscious mind, because the rational mind, which sifts and censors, is off duty while we sleep.

This dream was for Mary a frightening experience, but it also enabled her to experience some of her anger with her mother for dying, an anger that her conscious mind could not logically countenance. After all, her mother's death had been a tragedy for them both, which she knew rationally that her mother had fought hard to prevent.

What can also be unnerving about such dreams is that it can sometimes be difficult to wake up from them and separate them clearly from waking 'reality'. It helps to share such dreams with someone who is trusted not to be alarmed, shocked or dismissive.

Knowing that such experiences are normal in bereavement protects the dreamer from unfounded fears of insanity.

The violence of some of the feelings experienced in bereavement mirrors the violence implicit in death. Even the gentlest of deaths extinguishes the vital spark of life. Strong language reflects this: feeling 'torn', 'agonised', 'cut in two', 'tormented' 'tortured'. Fear is a very natural response to that kind of reality.

5. Guilt

Guilt is often an element in relationships between the living, so why should death remove it? The opportunities for guilt in bereavement pile up. There can be a host of regrets:

- Why didn't I spot his loss of weight?
- Why didn't I get her to see the doctor sooner?
- Why wasn't I more patient when he was ill?
- I could have done more to relieve her suffering, improved the quality of her life or even prevented her death.
- If I had known that this was going to happen, I would never have spoken to him like that: no wonder he was making so many mistakes those last few days.
- She was difficult to get on with, but I'll never forgive myself for not trying harder.

When negativity in relationships is high, guilt is often worse. The dead person can be idealised, stimulating even more guilt. Normal levels of guilt will not inhibit resolution but excessive levels may do.

The sense of having done wrong is widespread among the bereaved. Being the one still alive can contaminate the simplest and most innocent of life's pleasures. 'It's all very well for me to enjoy this, but it's never again going to be possible for him to have a jar of real ale or strawberries and cream or listen to a Mozart symphony or watch Leeds'.

Carl's grandfather spoke at the eight year old boy's funeral, after his tragic drowning in a canal. 'I loved that boy so much. He was so full of life, but it would never have done to have told him so, because youngsters can get to think too much of themselves if you're not careful. But now I wish I had told him somehow how much I loved him'.

The importance of expressing appreciation, affection and respect at work and at home is often most poignantly realised when someone's death makes it no longer possible. Sometimes there is also the wish to have cleared something up or to have said something that now can never be said. Whatever the reality behind the guilt, the need to feel the guilt and regret, and then to undergo the experience of forgiving oneself and accepting one's limitations is a crucial part of grieving for some people.

In a poor relationship the guilt may be especially focused on the fact that we have run out of time to improve things. A sense of relief that the person is no longer around can also fuel guilt in some people.

Lastly, guilt can interweave with or contribute or add to any of the other aspects of bereavement, such as depression, anger or fear. They may be thought of as self-indulgent, weak or sinful, depending on values, gender, culture and other conditioning. Bereavement sometimes takes the lid off powerful emotions that have hitherto, more or less, been successfully repressed.

Simon grew up with the view that anger and aggression were wrong, and avoided fights as a child. He was known as a peaceful and peace loving person. His girl friend was then tragically killed by a drunken motorist, and he grieved deeply for her, but with little anger. Such feelings were a waste of time in his book. Then one evening he was having a quiet drink with some friends, when a group of drunken youths started abusing him. His mind went blank at some point until he found himself being hauled off by one of them whom he had attacked so severely that the youth had to go to a hospital casualty department. This incident was the trigger for him to seek further support through his personnel manager. Previously Simon had reassured him that he was fine and was coping, despite some concern in the company that he was finding it hard to get back into the swing of work eight months after the accident.

Fortunately an understanding of the human response to loss can sometimes help us re-evaluate such a rejection of part of our feelings. Whatever our conditioning, we need the ability to feel without guilt, anger, depression and fear, in order to grieve.

6. Anger and Resentment

Fury can be acted out in uncontrolled violence, leading to some of the grievous bodily harm and murder that disfigures society, but fury also fuels the fight for justice and a better world.

Intrinsically therefore it is part of being human and needs to be understood, accepted, channelled and managed in a constructive way.

Anger is an integral part of most healthy grieving, even though it may be disguised. We can be angry on behalf of the person who has died for their loss of life and perhaps too for their suffering. Anger is for many a frightening emotion. It is consequently particularly important that bereaved people are helped to express it and to understand that it is a normal part of grieving. The venting of anger, without physically hurting anyone, can be a valuable means of relieving accumulated stress.

Anger can still feel very painful and is often difficult to express. It can seem inappropriate and even shameful. It is sometimes difficult to find a suitable target for one's anger, but a target may present itself or be found through transferring our feelings onto someone near at hand. Friends, colleagues, family or neighbours who gave less time than was needed; doctors, nurses, clergy or others in a caring role, who were inadequate or seemed so, can all become the object of our fury.

An employer can also be the target of anger, especially if it is thought that work was the cause of death. That this may be part of the grieving response does not, however, necessarily mean that there was no bullying or oppressive style of management operating. It is not acceptable to dismiss anger as just part of the grieving process as if that lets senior management off the hook about taking its cause seriously, irrespective of whether it is expressed formally in the form of a grievance.

The new General Manager came in to tighten up the place. A tough workaholic, who prided himself on his lack of sentimentality, he soon got to work on Jim, who was from the 'old school' of industrial relations: short on confrontation, long on building trust and two-way understanding. The GM assumed that Jim had been soft on the unions for many years and had conceded too much. Besides, he didn't like the way Jim usually left work at about 6 p.m. to be with his family or the youth club, to both of which he was devoted. Jim found it difficult to attend the GM's long evening meetings. He felt increasingly stressed with the unrelenting pressure from the GM. A month after redundancy, he became ill: a myeloma was diagnosed and he died six months later, aged 48. He took his illness with the same stoic forbearance with which he had struggled to tolerate and adjust to the GM's behaviour. His widow was aware that some cancer may be stress related. While a connection could not be proved, her anger sprang from her conviction that the GM had caused his death.

Nevertheless, many trades union representatives and human resource managers have been approached by staff bubbling over with rage. The fury may sometimes seem disproportionate to the incidents or behaviour that triggered it. Part of the skill that they must have is the ability to help the staff member cool down before helping them to decide whether pursuing the matter further is appropriate.

While anger is part of the bereavement process, it can also be a mask for grief, especially for those men conditioned to believe that anger is manly, whereas grief is not. Such men may need encouragement to express their underlying grief so that they can be purged of it. This applies in reverse. Some women have been brought up to think that anger is incompatible with femininity. They may unconsciously mask their resentment with grief and need help to acknowledge their anger directly and not only through tears.

We may also direct some of our resentment towards the deceased for dying, for not fighting harder, for leaving us to cope alone with so much. Although this anger may appear rational and consequently easier to admit in the case of suicide or carelessness, it can also be strongly felt where someone had no means of preventing their death. The question can still rumble away beneath the surface: did they really have to die, leaving us inadequately supported? Could they not have tried harder to fight death. This anger sometimes breaks the shell of our denial.

God may also become the focus of anger. Anger transcends superficial rationality in many ways: committed atheists can be as angry with the God they do not believe in as a more conventionally religious person. Even though innocent suffering is part of the human condition, as a result of natural and human disasters and the way diseases and accidents happen, people can still be affronted with God when they or someone close to them becomes a victim. The religious tradition is full of the struggle to reconcile belief in a loving God with suffering. Somehow suffering has to be understood as part of the divine purpose, from which God does not escape. Atheists, with struggles of their own, are glad to be off the hook of this one.

Anger, whatever the target, is a natural, if uncomfortable, response to the death of someone we care about. It is important that we are allowed and indeed encouraged to own it, without it being undermined by intellectual analysis. When anger is adequately expressed, we will usually come to understand which parts, if any, are rationally justified and which have been burned up in the fire of the moment.

Dylan Thomas (1952) wrote:

> Do not go gentle into that good night.
> Old age should burn and rave at close of day;
> Rage, rage against the dying of the light.

But the grief implicit in the anger bursts through in the final verse:

> Curse, bless me now with your fierce tears, I pray.

7. Depression

After the exhaustion of the earlier stages, bereavement usually causes us to sink into depression: uncertainty, lack of confidence, apathy and despondency. It can find expression in a desire to stay within the safety of our own home or with a few close friends and family. Absenteeism from work, poor concentration and decline in competence are also common symptoms of the depression of grief that often follows more obvious mourning. It often feels hard to stick close to people at this time, as they are as likely to stimulate a strong and impatient urge to try to move them on before they are ready. The pressure on colleagues to maintain goodwill and tolerance as well as output with someone underperforming can be tough. If the bereaved person is off work, it may be possible to get temporary extra help. But if they have returned and are not firing on all cylinders, colleagues need to be willing, understanding and flexible if they are to play their part in helping the bereaved person back to full functioning. Those who are marked by scars, bandages, plaster or crutches inspire easier empathy than those with the invisible wound of a broken heart.

> Give sorrow words. The grief that does not speak
> Whispers the o'er fraught heart, and bids it break.

So, in *Macbeth*, Shakespeare suggests the heart of grief that finds expression, not in the agitated energy of acute grief, but in whispers. Instead of the unreal optimism of denial, there is the bleakness in which any flicker of light at the end of the dark tunnel is extinguished. Apathy, despondency and despair are characteristic of times in which the long-term implications of loss begin to be realised. The physical exhaustion in grief is most in evidence, lowering morale even more. Lack of energy makes it doubly hard to maintain standards at work or at home. Self-care and personal appearance may deteriorate. The depressed person is likely to contributes minimally to relationships and needs to become more of a 'taker' than a giver. All of this will be more or less difficult, depending on how different it is to their previous behaviour.

> Andy's partner died 8 months ago and as his manager I made every allowance at the time. He seemed to be handling it well; but now I'm having second thoughts. He is pretty ungracious with everyone who supported him, and I am beginning to think that he is taking advantage of the situation and being a little too sorry for himself'. Andy's manager was making the common error that support for a bereaved colleague only needs to be relatively short term. Andy was still very much in the grip of grief and his behaviour gave all the indications of depression, a natural part of the process.

It was important for his manager to acknowledge that Andy's behaviour was atypical of him. It was an expression of some of his grief, which with good support rather than censure was more likely to work through until he could function again in a way that his manager wanted.

This sadness can be even more confusing in those with a general tendency towards depression. For them, bereavement can add an extra layer of sadness, which may make it especially hard to endure. Support for them may therefore be doubly important, even though their behaviour when bereaved may seem to vary less from their norm than the behaviour of those not subject to depression.

There are, in any case, times when it may feel harder to support the bereaved, and consequently when they are particularly prone to feelings of 'being let down'. The drama of death can keep the adrenaline going on both sides at first. When that runs out, the longer haul of mourning and support begin.

> Shirley wrote 'I never lost anyone really close to me until my father died, just eleven months ago. I knew sadness and pain before then but never as great or as lasting as I know now. Slowly my optimism and self-confidence are coming back; I lost them when he died. I know I will never be the same person I was before he died. It feels as if I have lost some of the magical power and strength he gave me simply by his being alive – I have lost a bit of

the immortality I had simply by knowing he existed somewhere on this earth'. Shirley was a dynamic person at work with responsibility for supervising and managing a team of 20, as well as being a mother of two young children. She felt that her energy was a crucial part of her effectiveness at work and home, and struggled with the loss of it during the 18 months after her father's death. She felt she was letting other people down as she struggled to regain her sense of who she was.

8. Loneliness

As the preoccupation with the dead person recedes, loneliness creeps in, especially for those left to live alone. Sexual loneliness sometimes leads to promiscuity and then to more guilt. In the earlier phases, there is a kind of psychological companionship, albeit painful, through the preoccupation with the one who has died. As this fades, the reality of life without the loved one becomes a further source of pain, as if the lonely heart of grief has been finally reached.

If the dead person was a living-in companion, there is a whole lifestyle to change. Everything previously undertaken together, from shopping and housework, to meals, weekends and holidays, must now be undertaken alone. The adjustment that is required is colossal, especially if they have been together for a long time. For some, such as many gay or lesbian couples, there is an added dimension to their pain, because their loss may not be acknowledged or even realised by others. Hence the crucial role gay support groups can play in this area.

The loneliness of those caring for a child or a disabled person, who subsequently dies, can also be especially intense. Much of the previous life had been so taken up with care that the resulting gap and emptiness may feel huge.

Loneliness can also be felt sexually, sometimes as an increase in libido. This can feel like betraying the person who has died and be an added source of unnecessary shame, instead of reflecting how sex was a channel for expressing love and a good deal besides. Loneliness is often most acute in bed.

It's two years now and it feels mostly a lot better than it used to, until I go to bed when the empty space still feels unbearable.

This need for closeness with another person, driven by great emotional need and power, can bring the recently bereaved all too easily into close relationships, which do not have the sure foundation to last. There is likely to be an element of searching (see above), sometimes at the simplest level. The bereaved person finds himself attracted to someone with characteristics that in some way remind him of the person who has died: for example, the same coloured hair or background. The object of their affection can feel let down and second best, when they realise this: 'she was not really interested in me, but rather just looking for another him'. If the subsequent relationship breaks down, more complications are added to the recovery process.

The wise friend or colleague will therefore be as cautious as the wise bereaved person in moving into a sexual relationship. There is a need to acknowledge that the person who is still attached to the one who has died may not yet be emotionally (as opposed to legally) free to attach him or herself to a new partner. The idea of clear sexual boundaries in relationships of various kinds is often particularly helpful in bereavement.

The loneliness of the bereaved in other relationships should not be underestimated. When a wife dies, for example, the support can easily be concentrated on her husband: her teenage children's loss by comparison is sometimes virtually ignored. Instead, friends and family are tempted to lecture them on how they need to support their father.

> When Dad died last year I was 15 and lived most of my life with my mates; or thought I did. The strange thing was that no adult asked me how I felt, or said to me that they were sorry. It felt as if my relationship with my father didn't exist or was nothing compared to him and my mum. I suppose it wasn't worth mentioning. Yet they all seemed to expect me to support her.

9. Resolution and Acceptance

Resolution is not a cessation of love or memories or even the pain of missing the deceased. Painful feelings have been sufficiently worked through to free the bereaved person for positive feelings towards the present and future, to function at or near their previous level They are also hopefully able to develop the trust necessary to form new, even intimate, relationships. Some elderly people, after a long partnership, cannot adjust and become stuck in depression. This is often linked to their feelings about their quality of life and a realisation that their own remaining time is too short for much of a new start; but that is not invariable, as the following case illustrates.

Gail was widowed after a long marriage in her mid 70s and lived independently for a further 25 years. Despite various battles with ill health, they were by her own admission happy years. Although she thought of her marriage with pride, her husband had been dominating and demanding. For her, being bereaved meant an element of sadness but also of freedom to take charge of her own life. The small decisions gave her great pleasure: when and what to eat and how to order her days and nights.

The conclusion of the process is reached when the bereaved start to experience times when they feel, a little at least, as they did before. Joyce Grenfell writing in 1980[3] expressed the hope implicit in this stage in her poem:

> If I should go before the rest of you
> Break not a flower nor inscribe a stone.
> Nor when I'm gone speak in a Sunday voice.
> But be the usual selves that I have known.
> Weep if you must.
> Parting is hell.
> But life goes on.
> So sing as well.

There are, however, dangers in this stage of the process. The 'tyranny' of positive thinking can suggest unrealistic goals: with a stiff upper lip and plenty of denial, we might soon be living a normal life again almost as if nothing has happened. But there are no short cuts in grieving.

Bereavement can often be a tragedy, the quality of our survival depending on our working through the pain. The reward may be peaceful acceptance for some, but sad or bitter resignation for others. It depends on many factors, including the level of independence in the relationship, the depth of affection and the meaning of death to the person affected.

10. Introjection – Internalising the Qualities of the Person who Has Died

In a relationship, often the 'marital fit' finds expression in the different skills and knowledge that we each bring to our relationships. One may be a good cook or driver or first aider or manager of the household accounts or gardener and end up doing or at least supervising and leading the work needed in those areas within the relationship. If that person dies, the other one has to do the work himself or find another way of getting it done, unless that area is just to be neglected. Although the idea has been expressed originally as that of 'marital fit', it might be better renamed 'relationship fit', as the process can operate in all kinds of close personal and working relationships, which are strengthened through a variety of complementary skills and attributes.

What is sometimes called 'introjection' can help a bereaved person move forwards. In this (usually unconscious) process, one member of a partnership internalises and perhaps acts out characteristics associated with the other. In absorbing aspects or the essence of the deceased, the bereaved person may take on some of their interests or even mannerisms. This process operates at many levels: the husband who has never boiled an egg becomes a competent cook. The wife who has never paid a bill develops confidence in domestic finances. Where this happens there is less danger of entering into an inappropriate second relationship as a means of getting a decent meal or escaping the anxiety of the unopened brown envelope. This process is not restricted to ex-partners. It is not unusual, for example, for an eldest child, especially of the same sex, to take on some aspects of the role of a deceased parent. An elder son may become more responsible, and perhaps take on some of his father's jobs around the house.

Introjection can also operate within a personality, although less obviously. A hitherto unsociable person develops socially after the death of their more outgoing partner, who previously 'covered that side of things'. Another person finds an interest in a subject in which their spouse had been knowledgeable.

Lily Pincus[4] put it: 'The mourning process involves the healing of a wound. Once the physical wound has been safely covered by healthy tissue, the process is completed and the patient does well to forget all about the injury. In mourning, however, the cause of the injury, the loss of an important person, must not be forgotten. Only when the lost person has been internalised and becomes part of the bereaved, a part which can be integrated with his own personality and enriches it, is the mourning process complete, and now the adjustment to a new life has to be made'.

Notes

1. Parry, Colin & Wendy, *Tim: An Ordinary Boy* (Hodder and Stoughton, 1994).
2. Lewis, C.S. *A Grief Observed*, (Faber & Faber, London, 1961)
3. Whitaker, A. (editor), *All in the End is Harvest: An Anthology for Those Who Grieve*, (DLT/Cruse, London, 1984).
4. Pincus, L. *Death and the Family: The Importance of Mourning*, (Faber, London, 1976).

7

Helping the Bereaved Person at Work

- Reticence and Openness at Work
- The Need for Managers to Know about Bereavement
- The Terminally Ill Member of Staff
- When Someone Dies
- Viewing the Body
- The Funeral
- Returning to Work after Someone Has Died
- The 'Cross Over to the Other Side' Response
- Practical Support
- Solidarity with the Bereaved

Given that death and bereavement are a proper concern for the workplace, the next consideration is how to help those at work who are passing through the stages of bereavement. It is useful to view this in relation to three situations:

1. When someone is dying.
2. When someone dies.
3. After someone has died.

All three situations are likely to be very charged emotionally. People act and react differently, but often with powerful feelings, whether or not they show them at work. If you are on the receiving end of the expression of a lot of distress, it does not necessarily mean that you have hurt the feelings of the other person or made matters worse. They were in all probability upset already: all you have hopefully done is to give them permission, perhaps unintentionally, to share how they feel. So long as your response is sensitive and respectful, they will hopefully feel supported. In the first of these situations 'when someone is dying', chapters 12 and 13 are particularly relevant, but this chapter concentrates on the issues facing a colleague who has been bereaved. Chapters 10 and 15 may also be relevant in their consideration of the practical tasks after someone has died and on funeral arrangements.

Reticence and Openness at Work

A useful way of looking at our own and other people's behaviour in a variety of situations is depicted in the Johari Window,[1] a well-known model highlighting four aspects of personality:

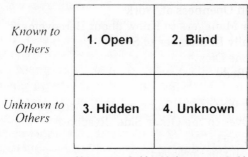

	Known to Self	Unknown to Self
Known to Others	**1. Open**	**2. Blind**
Unknown to Others	**3. Hidden**	**4. Unknown**

1. Openness. In this area, we and others know the impression we are giving.
2. Sometimes we are unaware and may have a Blind Spot: we leak out information about ourselves, our attitudes and thoughts unintentionally and without awareness. Others may have a better idea of what we are thinking than we do.
3. At other times part of us is Hidden, in that we conceal our behaviour, thoughts or feelings from other people, possibly deliberately.
4. We also have part of ourselves, which is Unknown and deeply hidden, to ourselves and to others.

The principle of the Johari Window is that if we open ourselves to others, through self-disclosure, and allow others to show us more of ourselves, through feedback, the Open area is enlarged at the expense of all the other three areas. This can promote honesty and understanding, which in turn increases trust, all of which strengthen relationships in such a way that we are more likely to work together effectively, whether we are building a team, a family or a friendship.

Openness is, however, not always desirable. Taken to the extreme it can lead to an inappropriate 'letting it all hang out', which may seem egotistical and result in us dominating situations with our own concerns, while others hardly have a chance to get a word in edgeways. It is sensible to assess with whom and in which situations openness is appropriate. Even then openness is for most people a matter of degree. Some people are very open to the point where they can come across as socially unskilled or insensitive: the gap between their brain and their mouth appears to be too short!

In bereavement we may talk without discernment to too many people, too often at the wrong times and too publicly. At times this may be unavoidable, if the power of our distress overwhelms us unexpectedly. A helpful colleague may respond flexibly and take us aside and give us a little time and support in order to share what is happening to us and then to recover enough to go back into a more public setting. We may be surprised that such an outburst can occur some time after the bereavement, triggered unexpectedly sometimes by the smallest thing, a chance remark or memory. Colin Parry wrote after the death of his 12 year old son in the Warrington bombing: 'You must be prepared for many, many weeks during which odd little events will trigger off irrational responses. I remember almost breaking down in public when I heard a tune that Tim had loved. You will be shaken with grief when you see your lost child's lookalike playing in the street.'[2]

We are constantly deciding, in small as well as large ways, how much truth to share and how much time to take sharing it in any given situation. This is so natural a part of human interaction that it often happens without thinking. It is a healthy and normal inhibition, by which we protect our vulnerability while hopefully being sensitive to others. Reticence, therefore, has an honourable place in good relationships. But reticence too can be taken to an extreme: constant repression and evasiveness are as unhelpful as the opposite end of the spectrum. We are looking for the right balance for any particular situation on the continuum between:

Repression/Suppression – Reticence – Openness – Let it all hang out!

Some people may appear to be evasive at work and not to want to talk about their bereavement, because it is too painful and they are anxious that they may become too emotional and even more distracted from their work than they are already. Or they may just assume, without checking it out or being told otherwise, that the death (and bereavement) taboos operate in their work culture. They may fear that they will be judged as incapable of handling pressure, if they appear overly affected by their bereavement, and therefore not ready for a promotion, a merit award or an important assignment. As we have already seen, the natural inhibitions that lie behind reticence do not function reliably when newly bereaved. The colleague may judge that they may not be able to control their emotions, if they allow the lid to come off, even a little. On the other hand, they may believe none of this but want to try to use work as a reprieve from grief by focusing on their job, knowing that at home their bereavement will be dominating their time and attention.

> Darren's baby had died tragically when only 6 months old. There was a great surge of sympathy for him after the event from the other staff in the insurance company claims office, not least from a couple of women also with young babies. Their sympathy began to wear thin, however, when after a couple of days back at work, he returned to his routine of having a football 'kick around' with some of the other lads during his lunch break. How could he if he really cared, they felt; but we often need to begin to normalise our life with breaks from our grief. This was a good way for Darren to do it, even though privately he was going through hell in a way some of his colleagues never realised.

The bereaved staff member may not be receiving much support at home. It may not be available because he or she may live on their own and be relatively isolated, or they may live with a partner or other people and still be relatively isolated. Bereavement can be one of many factors that apparently trigger the break up of a marriage. A relationship that is already rocky is one in which partners are often unwilling or incapable of offering each other support. Even in a good relationship, some find it hard to receive support. Colin Parry again: 'The first thing that the families of the dead must do is to feel for each other. You have to close ranks and make allowances for each other. You see, my wife and I learned that people do not grieve according to schedules and timetables. There are wild and irrational mood swings. There were times when I was overcome by grief and anger and she appeared calm and controlled. There were times when the raw emotion was hers, and I was numb and frozen.'[3]

The situation may be exacerbated by denial, which (as discussed in chapter 6) is hopefully temporary. As a consequence, managers and colleagues need to respect reticence, by not pushing the person to talk when they do not want to, while making it clear that they are more than willing to listen, if at some point that might help. They need to show that they are interested because they care about how the person is doing. They want to know how they are, out of concern rather than prurient or gossipy curiosity.

The Need for Managers to Know about Bereavement

Key staff involved need to have some basic information about the bereavement process, especially those with no personal experience so that they are able to consider what the person concerned might be experiencing. That person may be a member of staff who is either terminally ill or living with, or closely related to, someone who is dying. The key staff may include the immediate line manager and supervisor, the shop steward or staff representative, the personnel or human resources (HR) manager and probably other close colleagues.

Providing support is demanding if it is to be done well. There are two prerequisites. First, the immediate line manager needs the personal support of another person. This can be anyone with warmth, emotional maturity and an understanding of the bereavement process. It need not be that person's line or personnel or HR manager.

Secondly, it is important for the manager to be aware if he or she has any residual grief from another source still to resolve. Left alone, this 'unfinished business' might impede the manager's ability to help the person concerned. If there is unresolved grief to attend to, extra support may be needed. There is no objective test for unresolved grief, but a close bereavement in the past two years is a reasonable basis for a closer look.

Alec's father died after a long illness, having been told four days beforehand that he would not see Christmas, even though that was six months away. Until that point Christmas with his grandchildren had been his next goal, but when that was taken away, it was as if he just let go of life. Alec and his father had maintained a close friendship and companionship, cemented by their devotion to Rugby football. They had both played for the same club, which they supported and shared regular pilgrimages to Twickenham, which sometimes included their wives and Alec's two children. With Alec working away from home his father often took the children to their various sporting commitments, giving them plenty of encouragement.

Alec had always been a rock in the family, supporting others whenever they had difficulties of one kind or another. They knew he was devastated by the loss of his father, but felt that they could not get near him. His own conditioning had taught him how to give but not to receive support. He felt that, as a man, he had always to display invulnerable strength within the family, making the others feel helpless and distant from him at a time when they needed to feel close. The children, especially his son, felt confused, because it was as if Alec was not as upset as they thought he would be and as they felt themselves. Perhaps he did not really love granddad after all?

His manager, being an observant man and having worked closely with Alec for over 10 years, suspected some of this, especially when he noticed the uncharacteristic formality within the family at the funeral. Soon afterwards, he asked Alec to come and see him to check how things were and what kind of time off that he might be needing to sort out the loose ends of his father's house. He asked him how things were in the family and how it was for his children in particular, knowing how close they had been to their grandfather.

It was the first time Alec had opened up about it and he talked for over an hour about the whole situation, and a good deal about the kind of man his father had been. Towards the end his manager sowed the seed by asking him if he had talked to his children like this or asked them to share their memories. Alec hadn't because he might get upset. 'So what,' replied his manager, 'all it will do is to show them what their granddad meant to you. It would be very strange if they thought you didn't care about his death.' A couple of months later, Alec told his manager that that conversation was a turning point for him in getting some insight into what he was going through and understanding of how he might support his family, by letting them support him. That support had to be a two-way street.

The Terminally Ill Member of Staff

The terminally ill person has two separate clusters of needs. One is the need for effective symptom relief and care (emotional and practical). The other is the need for time with friends and loved ones while there is still the opportunity. Line managers should regard it as one of their responsibilities to check out whether these needs are being met.

As far as quality time with others is concerned, it may not be helpful only to grant leave when there is a crisis: it can be very important to spend time together on good days too. This is where a flexible approach to leave entitlement by an enlightened line manager can be crucial.

The person's illness should be acknowledged by the line manager at frequent intervals. To establish the current situation, open, non-threatening questions can be used, asked with empathy and discretion. In particular the line manager will want to:

- stress that the company remains committed to the person concerned, and their family, if appropriate, as people and not just as units of production;
- reassure the person that the company understands and accepts that the person's work effectiveness is likely to be affected.

If powerful analgesics are being taken to control pain, it may be necessary to relieve the employee of certain tasks, such as those which require intense concentration, involve safety issues or are physically arduous. But managers and occupational health staff will need to exercise much tact to avoid creating a sense of uselessness. Colleagues are usually only too pleased to help out temporarily by taking on additional or alternative work, if they understand the reasons. There is a fine balance to be struck here between being open with them and respecting the staff member's desire for confidentiality. It is usually best to agree with him or her what it is appropriate to say, to whom and under what circumstances.

Periodic, informal discussions between manager and staff member can be very helpful in monitoring how things are going. Essential for such meetings will be:

- adequate time;
- a private setting, with comfortable chairs and a box of tissues available;
- the willingness to hear how things really are;
- the capacity to accept strong emotions (including tears) without embarrassment on anxiety;
- the timing: preferably before a meal break or going home time.

Returning immediately to the working area may be difficult if painful feelings have surfaced and been shared.

The temptation in such a meeting to divert or interrupt tears or anger or to pretend that they do not exist, for example, needs to be avoided. The manager has to reach the point in his own development where he is either comfortable with the expression of strong feelings or at least can cope with them so that he does not give out subtle or not so subtle messages that he wants the person to become less emotional. This discomfort may be acted out by fleeing or getting rid of the member of staff:

'I will go and get you a glass of water/cup of coffee ...'
'Why don't you go and talk to personnel ...'
'Would you like to go to the ladies until you feel a bit better ...'
'Perhaps you would like me to leave you for a while until you feel a little better ...'

All of these responses give out the message that this is not the manager's business and is possibly wasting his time, although he is prepared to talk in a sensible way, if the member of staff can present his difficulties or problem in a coherent way. Whereas what the staff member may need is the opportunity to share his or her feelings that may feel confused so that they can reach the point when they are able to articulate their needs.

The acceptance of how the person is feeling is often best communicated by a combination of active listening and reflecting the person's feelings back in your own words. For example, the manager might say 'it feels very painful, George,' or 'I can see how much you care about him'. The agenda for such a meeting will be to check out how things are both at work and at home, what the member of staff's current needs are and what, if anything, the company might do differently to help.

When Someone Dies

When someone dies, condolence and support need to be offered immediately to the bereaved person, whether it is a staff member who has died or a partner, next-of-kin or another close relative or friend. Circumstances will help determine the best method – telephone, personal visit or letter. If in doubt, risk being more, rather than less, personal. But bear in mind also that it may be the time to stand back a little, given that the crucial time for the company will be during the transition back to work (in the case of a bereaved person) and when the immediate family and friends are beginning to relinquish their close support.

It is important to find out early, however, whether the bereaved person does in fact have family and friends to provide support. If emigration, death or a family feud has removed them, the organisation may be best placed to fill such a gap. Where employers have encouraged mobility, and therefore contributed

indirectly to breaking up the extended family, it may be especially fitting if they make an early response.

If that is the case, an appropriate person can, on behalf of the
company, support them through the practical tasks that need
doing, and in doing so sensitively, also provide emotional support
in their grief. The checklist on pp. 197ff or some of it may be
helpful to the member of staff, even if the manager uses it for his
or her own guidance

Viewing the Body

Except in parts of Northern England and Ireland, it is less
common now in Britain for the body to remain at home between
death and the funeral. That custom enabled family and friends to
spend unhurried time with the body, adjusting to the new reality
and taking their leave together or alone. Another custom is to
remove the coffin lid during the funeral service, and for
mourners to be invited to view the body on their way out of the
church. Unusual except in some black communities, it helps
mark the farewell and the beginning of a new stage in which the
person lives on, apart from the body, in the hearts and minds of
family and friends.

Although the body is no longer the abode of the person, we
relate to each other in and through our bodies. It is false therefore to pretend that we should have no deep feelings towards a
person's body, once the person is dead. To spend time with the
body can help mourners at their own pace to separate their love
and attachment for the person from the person's body, which in
their lifetime have been inextricably interwoven.

Whether or not to view the body needs to be a personal decision. Some have done so and wished they had not, because their
final memory of the person is a distorted image of death, possibly
made more difficult if the person has been made up and laid out
in an alien environment. Martha and her family found great
comfort in seeing her father's body laid out in his own bed for the
days before the funeral, allowing people to say their farewells in
the familiar surroundings of his own home. In contrast, Virginia
Ironside wrote about the death of her father: 'Then there was
seeing my father in the Chapel of Rest and wondering what he
would have thought of the extraordinary hair style the
embalmers had given him.'[4]

The physical reality of death is not necessarily more

distressing than the imagined reality. Except where there has been serious facial injury, being with the dead body can help in coming to terms with the reality of death and moving through the healing process of mourning. The body changes physically, so soon becoming pallid and cold, which for many seems to make it easier to accept that the person is no longer there.

The Funeral

Colleagues need to be informed of the death sensitively and in accordance with the wishes of the bereaved, so that they can contribute to the groundswell of support needed at such a critical time. Unless requested otherwise, attendance at the funeral should be encouraged. The employer will probably want to be officially represented and a turnout of those who knew the deceased well can be very supportive to the family, so long as attendance is genuine and voluntary. There should also be a letter of condolence from a senior manager, preferably the most senior person in the organisation who knew the bereaved or deceased personally. In chapter 15, funerals and 'rites of passage' are considered in more detail.

Support needs to be person-centred. If the grieving person wants to be left largely alone, this should be respected, with the proviso that someone with counselling experience should keep an eye on the situation. Some monitoring is advisable, because, although a degree of privacy is natural in grief, complete isolation is rarely the best basis for mourning. It can lead to such an overwhelming weight of grief that the person subsequently has a breakdown or becomes suicidal. The person's desire for privacy must be balanced against such risks.

Returning to Work after Someone Has Died

When a person returns to work after the death of a friend or relative, colleagues are often embarrassed about whether to say anything and, if so, what? In general, if you have any kind of personal relationship with the grieving person, you should acknowledge their loss openly and promptly. The quality of your relationship may be impaired if this does not happen. Somehow the loss, sadness or tragedy needs to be made explicit for healing to occur. It should not be undermined by a cheery 'look on the bright side', which is a form of denial.

The first reference to the grief should be private and as natural as possible. It need not be in a separate office but should be discreet; a warehouse, corridor, factory bench or open-plan office may be perfectly adequate, as long as the conversation is private.

The 'Cross Over to the Other Side' Response

The worst we can do for each other in these circumstances is to cross over to the other side of the work street, allowing our embarrassment, indifference or mistaken sense of sensitivity to cause people to leave the bereaved alone. Suffering is seldom minimised by avoiding the subject of death. It may be increased, because the person concerned feels more isolated. This response is all too frequent and hurtful. A wise way of avoiding denial is to afford the bereaved a settling-in period (a few minutes or hours), and then actively to seek the person out, rather than leaving an encounter to chance.

> On Bill's return to work after his mother's premature death, he found a note on his desk querying his time off. The personnel officer did not know about his bereavement, and subsequently was covered in confusion and embarrassment and apologised to Bill for what had happened. Nevertheless, Bill felt hurt and angry that he had had to sort out with his line manager, on his first day back, the muddle over his compassionate leave.

What to Say?

When you do meet, what do you say? What is usually unhelpful is to say anything which minimises the loss: it is not for you to reassure or look on the bright side. Examples of such well-meaning but inappropriate greetings to bereaved members of staff on their return to work include:

I'm sorry your father died, but ...

- I believe that it was expected;
- it must have been a relief for him / for you;
- he had a good innings;
- it means you can start to look forward now;
- we all have to go sometime.

To 'reconnect' with the person, say something simple and genuine which expresses, directly or indirectly, how you feel.

- I'm very sorry about Helen.
- You've been in my thoughts a lot these last few days.
- Tom, I can't find the words to tell you how sorry I am.
- He was a great person: it's a terrible loss.
- If you ever feel like talking, you know where I am.
- Why don't you bring the children over for a meal at the weekend.

But more important than the words are your concern and compassion. These will be felt and will shine through, since the person will be especially sensitive during this phase of bereavement. Do not expect it to feel comfortable: your discomfort may be an indication that you are being genuine and not putting on an emotional mask.

Practical Support

The relevance of the last example above is that it implies emotional help but explicitly offers practical help. In some cultures, the extended family and neighbours take responsibility for all meal preparation for the bereaved during their first month of mourning. If people feel able to accept such help, it is excellent to provide it. Work colleagues will know more than they first realise about practical ways of helping: transport for children, partners and elderly dependants, tidying the garden before the funeral... It may also be supportive to offer to go with the person to register the death, and to help sort out any urgent financial matters.

What happens once the person has returned to work and the grief has been explicitly acknowledged? Some colleagues will breathe a sigh of relief that that is over and lapse into the 'ignore' mode. But however well disguised it may be, grieving will continue long after the return to work. This may be uncomfortable to be near: another person's loss can remind us of our own past griefs as well as our human vulnerability and mortality.

Solidarity with the Bereaved

On a day-to-day basis we may live as if death was not part of our personal reality. That illusion is undermined when death gets uncomfortably close to us. If we want good human relationships, we have to live with our discomfort and acknowledge our solidarity with the bereaved. Practically, this will involve action such as:

- periodically ask how they are;
- continue to be prepared to make time for them
- offer attentive listening;
- give them 'permission' to talk or not;
- review what practical support might be appropriate as time passes.

A Check List for the Bereaved Person Returning to Work

DO

- Let yourself experience the pain of grief.
- Share how you feel with those (including colleagues) with whom you feel safe.
- Allow yourself more rest than usual: bereavement can be very tiring.
- Avoid heavy drinking (or illegal drugs) to dull the pain.
- Be cautious about major decisions in the early months.
- Expect the need to talk about your loss to continue for longer than you might expect.
- Break yourself in gently and gradually after a discussion with your manager.
- Try and be open about the kind of support that you want (and don't want).

DON'T

- Try to avoid the pain.
- Be ashamed of your feelings – or tears.
- Fight the need to talk about it over and over again.
- Return to work until you feel you are ready.
- Take on new tasks or responsibilities too quickly.
- Be surprised if your concentration is affected.
- Be surprised if you have vivid and grief dreams.
- Be ashamed of your grief: it's a consequence of your involvement and love.

A Checklist for Colleagues When a Bereaved Person Returns to Work

DO

- Respect their reticence and their openness.
- Acknowledge the loss. Care more about the person than your own embarrassment.
- Encourage the person to talk, if they want to.
- Enable people to cry without loss of safety or self respect.
- Reassure that very powerful, vivid and unfamiliar feelings and dreams are a normal part of grieving.
- Check whether close colleagues know of the bereavement
- Check whether the bereaved wants others to be informed (who and how?)
- Acknowledge important anniversaries suitably and sensitively (deaths as well as births, weddings etc.).
- Discourage people from taking major decisions (e.g. job change, house move) early in the bereavement.

DON'T

- Pressurise them to get on with work if it is not essential.
- Minimise the impact of the loss.
- Reassure, when what's needed is permission to share grief.
- Limit the time in which support is given.
- Expect bereaved colleagues to be 'back to normal' quickly.
- Let your embarrassment stop you offering support.

Notes

1. Luft, J. and Ingham, H. *The Johari Window: A Graphic Model of Human Relations*, (University of California, Los Angeles, Extension Office, Western Training Laboratory in Group Development, 1995).

2. Parry, Colin 'Grief, anger, yes. But don't be poisoned by hatred' (*DailyMail*, London 17 August, 1998).

3. Ibid.

4. Ironside, Virginia 'On a voyage without my father' (*The Times*, London, 29 July 1992).

8

Sudden Death at Work

- When Someone Dies at Work
- Accidents and Murders
- Police Statement
- Guidelines after a Traumatic Event
- The Initial Visit by the Line Manager
- Debriefing by a Trained Team
- Responding to Anger
- Support Options
- Follow-Up by the Line Manager
- Voluntary One-to-One Counselling
- A Visit from 'Top' Management
- The General Stress Reaction
- Taking Care of Yourself

When Someone Dies at Work

If someone dies at work, whether a colleague, customer or supplier, the event inevitably and rightly has a powerful impact. How that impact is managed is crucial to the way staff can cope. If it is handled badly, it can cause unnecessary longer term difficulties for staff, quite apart from alienating them from a management they may perceive as inadequate, uncaring or both. If the person has committed suicide, the level of stress on those remaining is likely to be even greater. This is considered in particular in chapter 14, Choosing When to Die: Suicide and Euthanasia.

In some work settings, death is to be expected. Even in hospitals or a hospice, the death of a colleague or a friend can be as devastating as in other workplaces. The humanity of staff is a crucial element in their ability to help others in their dying and bereavement. Their own vulnerability means that they are as much in need of support when they are directly bereaved as anyone. War is another extreme example of a workplace where death not only happens and is sought, but for others not for yourself. Good nurses, doctors or members of the ambulance, fire or police services sometimes inevitably struggle with guilt because they feel that they could have done more to prevent someone's death. That guilt is a necessary part of real care and commitment, even though the guilt has to be managed or worked through so that it does not become incapacitating.

Whilst the guilt of a man or woman on 'active service' may be similar in relation to the death of a comrade, the guilt may be more complex over a human being they may have killed because he/she was temporarily assigned the role of enemy.

After the Gulf War, research[1] indicated that American marines being treated for Post Traumatic Stress Disorder commonly suffered from the following symptoms:

Sleep disturbance	(41 %)
Hyper-irritability	(38 %)
Hyper-alertness	(36 %)
Emotional numbing	(28 %)
Intrusive thoughts or flashbacks	(23 %)
Family or interpersonal problems	(22 %)

Accidents and Murders

Deaths resulting from accidents and murders produce the added agony of the feeling that they were unnecessary and caused by human folly or wickedness. They happen to people irrespective of their health and age and, therefore, generate the strongest feelings among the survivors. Over 22,000 people have been killed at work as a result of accidents in the past 30 years in the UK.[2] If the employer is found to be grossly negligent, a prosecution for corporate manslaughter may be recommended by the Health and Safety Executive after its investigation, although this is very rare. The Crown Prosecution Service accepts such cases even more rarely. What is more usual is a prosecution under Health and Safety legislation. The time taken by and the delays in these investigations themselves are an added source of stress. If all of this takes, for example, two years, the bereavement process can be slowed down: the bereaved are kept in a sort of limbo.

Calculated risks in economising on equipment and/or training have been estimated as a cause for about 60% of fatal accidents at work.[3] The inevitable anger that people normally feel in bereavement becomes reinforced if the employing organisation is believed to have caused it, because they were incompetent or did not care enough about their employees. For those who are left, there may be a strong desire for justice to be done. It may be fuelled in part by anger and a desire for revenge but also by their commitment to the person whose life has been taken away. There is a need to make sense of their death and find some good in the evil, perhaps in helping to prevent such tragedies in future, so that the person may be thought of as not having died completely in vain.

> On 16 July 1990, 24-year-old Jan Leadbetter fell to his death down an unguarded shaft on a construction site in central London, nine months after the death of Brian Billington, who fell down another unguarded shaft on the same site. At the inquest, the jury returned a verdict of accidental death, leaving relatives devastated and furious, especially after the coroner reportedly refused to accept the possible relevance of the earlier accident. The Construction Safety Campaign has organised pickets in recent years outside inquests to raise media and public awareness of the issues.[4]

Survivors of accidents can be helped, in a bizarre kind of way, if they have a visible injury which can heal. It is like a badge of injury, which others can see and acknowledge. Apparently 'getting off' in a situation when others have died can be a cause of guilt as well as relief, especially if the survivor saw or was with some of those who perished. (When there are serious facial injuries the above points do not apply.) Survivors with no injury, on the other hand, can feel very traumatised; but their wounds are invisible to those without awareness or with little empathic imagination.

Police Statement

If a statement is needed in the case of a death in suspicious circumstances, the police will generally want to take it as soon as possible after the incident, because facts can so easily become distorted over time, particularly in repeated telling. The sensitive taking of a statement can help catch suspects and also reduce the level of trauma by providing some scope for emotional release. But that it is not the officer's main aim and they may, in asking searching questions, come over as critical. The procedure can appear insensitive and be upsetting. Suggest that a colleague be with the member of staff during the interview, so that any necessary support can be provided during it and especially afterwards.

Guidelines after a Traumatic Event

Some general guidelines have been produced by Gary Mayhew[5] in identifying eight useful points to consider in the event of a potentially traumatic event, some of which may be useful in thinking about appropriate responses to a sudden death at work. Not all sudden deaths at work are sufficiently dramatic to attract media interest, in which case item 3 will be irrelevant; but all the other items are at least worthy of consideration, even if some of them are not necessarily acted upon:

1. Be aware of staff who have suffered other traumas; they may experience the old distress, compounded by the latest trauma.
2. Anyone pregnant or with a relevant pre-existing medical condition should see their general practitioner as soon as possible.
3. Encourage staff to telephone home before the event becomes publicised through the media.
4. Inform absent staff of the event, as this can spare them the shock of hearing about it from other sources or arriving at work without prior knowledge.
5. Ensure a co-ordinated, sensitive management response.
6. Expect short-term reduced efficiency from staff, including those who appear to be on the periphery.
7. Encourage (but do not compel) all staff to return to work the following day, even if they only perform light duties.
8. Arrange the debriefing, if possible, within 48 hours of the incident.

One Friday Bob witnessed the death of a colleague at work some miles from their base. They had worked together for over a year. It took him an hour to summon help and get a doctor to the scene, who confirmed Jack's death. Bob helped get the body back to base, where his team leader found him sitting in a state of shock. The team leader checked that Bob had been with Jack, told him that he would have to answer questions in the investigation, but that meanwhile he should get back home and get some rest. Presumably this was well intentioned, but the team manager never gave Bob a chance to say what had happened, to talk about how he felt or to debrief. He didn't know that Bob's parents, with whom he lived, had gone off on a week's holiday the day before. So Bob went back to an empty house and a very long and lonely weekend, which he passed in a nightmarish state of confusion.

Twenty years later, Bob had been promoted to a job as a personnel manager, which on the whole he did excellently; but he found supporting staff after a bereavement or an accident incredibly stressful. He sensed that in that area, he was considered to be a little inhuman and rigid. It felt as if that accident had happened yesterday. A counselling skills course Bob attended gave him more insight into how he had got stuck. It also provided an opportunity for him to talk through and to detoxify what had happened to him, as well as to Jack, so many years before.

Bob's team leader had, typically in those days, been given no briefing or training on how to support staff in such circumstances. Evidence is now emerging about what to expect after a traumatic event at work, especially if it is handled poorly. Staff may be distracted, demotivated and find it hard to work effectively or even to work at all. This may show up in levels of absenteeism and sickness. Incidents of alcohol or other drug related problems may increase, along with inter-personal conflict and unpredictable disruption.

A disaster may be on a small scale, but no less devastating in its impact (albeit on a small number of people, perhaps especially on an individual, like Bob). Or it may be much larger, as in the case of a terrorist attack or a natural disaster: fires, train crashes, raids, bombings, kidnappings or malicious attacks, which can all result in people dying or being very seriously injured. Increasingly good employers have their own contingency plan, so that they know what to do if the worst happens. The plan needs to be formulated and followed through so that key people are clear what is expected of them and sufficiently coached and trained, so that they can fulfil those expectations. Such a plan needs to have three core elements:

- The immediate support of staff – practical and emotional
- Debriefing by a team trained in appropriate counselling skills
- A follow up period of voluntary one-to-one counselling over a period of three weeks in the first instance.

The Initial Visit by the Line Manager

The immediate support of the staff is often best undertaken by a line manager, who would usually be the next most senior manager in the structure above the manager directly involved in the incident. As the company's representative, he or she needs to communicate the message that they and the company are primarily concerned with the welfare of staff at this stage. This is so much more important than physical damage to property or the loss of money that the latter may hardly be mentioned in the initial visit, at least by the manager. That is not to say that he or she will not need to listen to staff concern about what has been damaged or taken, not least if they have taken a pride in keeping their workplace in good order. That concern is primarily demonstrated by the quality of the manager's listening, through the way he asks about what happened, how they are and how they feel.

Talking can help take the pressure off, hence the importance of the manager being prepared to listen as the staff members tell him what happened in their own way. Check out how they feel and what their worries and concerns are. Some of these the manager may be able to do something practical about in the short term, but it may be as important to show that the staff member has been heard accurately and with respect by acknowledging what they have said and how they feel. If staff are reassured too quickly, it can leave the impression that what they have said is being minimised and not taken seriously.

Beware of humour. A well intentioned remark meant to break the ice or the tension can easily backfire and be experienced as insensitive or uncaring. That is not to deny that humour may be used as a way of coping by those involved and can be a helpful way of breaking the tension and expressing the relief that they have survived. Laughter itself can be very therapeutic. The visiting manager needs to acknowledge that the funny side is not the whole picture as well as acknowledging and perhaps even joining in the laughter.

The manager demonstrates care or the lack of it through what he does or does not do, for example, by organising transport home for staff who may be upset or in shock and not pressuring people back to work quickly. The manager provides someone, if appropriate, to provide support while the police take statements or if the staff member goes to hospital. He or she gives permission for people to take the time they need to recover in their own way, which also fits with business needs. Time taken by staff in the short term is likely to result in the normalising of the situation more quickly in the longer run and their return to full motivation and productivity.

Lastly, the manager needs to be ready to give some information about their possible response, that for example it would be very normal if they find themselves reacting strongly, once they are out of shock, 2 or 3 days after the incident. The information will be designed to help people know what to expect: how normal what seem like abnormal responses are in an abnormal situation. The manager also needs to explain what will happen next, such as health and safety or police procedures, if relevant, and also what follow up support will be forthcoming.

The importance of this initial support by the manager is reinforced in one company by making it a disciplinary offence for an area manager not to visit a branch within 12 hours of any raid, whether or not anyone was physically hurt.

In summary, the aims of the initial visit by the line manager are to:

- find out how people are by asking and listening well;
- ensure immediate practical help is offered and in place, if relevant;
- offer and give information that may be useful;
- prepare staff for follow up, including the support that he and the company will provide for them.

For the manager to undertake this role effectively, he or she needs to have access to a supportive human resources or line manager or counsellor, who will assist him prepare for his visit, if there is time, and certainly to debrief him after it – face to face or by telephone.

Peter Twist, a former senior officer in the Metropolitan Police, writes of an incident in the police station, which he line managed at the time:

> Dave was a much-loved and respected police officer who had retired, after completing his service, to an administrative post in the Crime Support Unit of the sister police station where he had served for many years. Although he was still well known to his former colleagues, he was now particularly close to the other members of his office with whom he worked on a daily basis.
>
> His daily routine was to start work at about 7 a.m. and prepare for investigating the crimes reported overnight. This routine was dramatically interrupted when, at about 7.45 a.m., Dave became suddenly unwell and collapsed with what was, and gave all the appearances of being, a massive heart attack. Help from colleagues was quickly summoned and an ambulance immediately called.
>
> A male and female police officer, who had returned to the station after patrolling in a police car, gave first aid and the agitated wait for the ambulance began. After 5 minutes it was

clear that Dave was dying and no satisfactory time of arrival of the ambulance could be ascertained. For better or for worse, the two officers decided to get Dave into their police car and drive straight to the nearest hospital.

The frenzied dash to the hospital began, with one of the officers doing all she could in the rear seat to keep Dave alive. Sadly, all her efforts were unsuccessful with the hospital casualty staff acknowledging defeat and pronouncing that Dave had been dead on arrival.

Back at work, the majority of staff had started to arrive at 8.30 a.m. to be greeted by the dreadful news. Disbelief, shock and horror ran through the police station: rumours abounded and, into the middle of this vortex of emotions, the two exhausted and deeply shocked officers returned.

Dave's next-of-kin was the companion with whom he had been living since the break-up of his marriage and a woman well known to many of the staff. To inform her of the news, the two officers insisted on visiting her personally, a gesture which, though difficult for them, gave reciprocal comfort and a sense of reality to them all.

As the officer in charge of the police station, I naturally attended the office at once as soon as I was informed and spoke to all concerned. Returning to my office, I telephoned our Occupational Health Department and, within an hour, trained staff arrived and started an immediate debrief. Even at this early stage, their sensitive ears picked up the seeds of recrimination, criticism and misinformation and a formal de-briefing session was arranged for all who wished to attend the following day.

This was invaluable in addressing the issues mentioned above and was especially appreciated by the two officers, who were able to give their colleagues a full and moving account of what they had done and why. In addition, care was taken to address the concerns of night duty staff.

Dave's funeral was held a week later and provided a significant tribute to and celebration of a lifetime of public service and companionship, unmarred by whispers of innuendo and condemnation.

Peter Twist spoke to the officers some time afterwards to see how they were doing in relation to the whole incident. The male officer appeared to have capably survived one more of the traumatic incidents, which had already peppered his career. His female colleague was more reflective: 'I feel privileged to have been able to give what I hope was some assistance to a colleague in his dying moments'.

Debriefing by a Trained Team

The staff group debriefing is designed to enable affected and involved staff to share some of what they have experienced. This in turn helps to normalise what they are going through, and promotes an environment of mutual understanding and support, in which they can (without being compelled) talk with each other about the incident and its aftermath, both for them as individuals and as a group. The debriefing will operate at a factual and practical as well as at a 'feeling' level. This procedure will allow staff to discuss any worries about the incident, such as safety arrangements, first aid or response times. It will also be another chance to talk about future support options that are available.

It is often good to have someone to do this from outside the management structure. In the case above trained specialists from Occupational Health came in. Alternatively human resource colleagues may be able to take this on, although specialist counsellors, external to the company, may also be a good choice. It is important, if at all possible, not to start until the whole group is present. On the other hand, if someone can only be seen at home or in hospital, a visit needs to be made but limited to caring for the staff member rather than a full debriefing. An invitation can be made for it to take place at an appropriate later date.

The group debriefing is a combination of input and facilitating staff to listen to each other. The facts of the incident are the starting point; and then different peoples' different perspectives on what happened and the impact on them in terms of how they have felt and been since. The staff are encouraged to tell each other as well as the debriefer what has happened on a number of levels. They may have different views about what happened and also the impact it made and is making on them. Some or all of them may need to express their anger, guilt, fear or disappointment. To do that may make others feel less isolated, as they realise that they are not necessarily the only ones feeling the way they do. It is important that the debriefer does not respond defensively to anger, but allows it to be expressed.

Without such a debriefing, some staff may feel that everyone else is less affected than they are, which can become a source of resentment towards the others for not apparently really caring about the person who has died. Although the company may well learn something useful for future planning or reference, the debrief is primarily a vehicle for staff support.

The input would often include something about the normal

responses and reactions to trauma, including some of the private symptoms, such as nightmares or seemingly irrational fears and anxieties that may worry some people greatly. They can lead to them assuming that they are signs that they are not 'hacking it' or coping, and be drawn into premature decisions that they will have to leave. Staff need to be told that they may experience different, possibly even stronger, feelings at a later stage, and not to be surprised: it is normal. That is why it is good to keep an open mind about follow up support, even if they feel it is not necessary now.

Lastly any suggestions made by those involved in the debriefing, as a group or by individuals, need to be seen to being taken seriously with a promise to think further about or to investigate their feasibility. Equally promises in the heat of the emotion to make changes, which cannot subsequently be delivered, need to be avoided. Feedback is essential. The debriefer must say that he or she will come back to them or ensure that someone else more appropriate does. Then the debriefer needs to ensure that they do within a reasonable period. Suggestions made at such a time, even if they are apparently small or even trivial, may carry the significance and emotional power of possibly preventing such a death in the future. That is why they need to be taken so seriously.

Responding to Anger

A representative may be on the receiving end of some anger, which may feel displaced. If the debriefing with the group or an individual has been well done, such safety will have been established for people to express how they feel if they wish. Others may be in such a volatile state that they cannot control how they feel, even if they want to. Either way the debriefer needs to receive the anger constructively. The following check list may help:

- Relax yourself before the debriefing as far as is possible
- Listen actively
- Try to understand how the person/people feel
- Remember that the anger may be what is on top, but other feelings may lie below the surface, such as fear
- Acknowledge the anger you sense, using reflection
- Remember that there is likely to be some truth in the anger, however irrationally it is expressed

- Don't argue back or respond aggressively by raising your voice
- Don't expect to resolve the problem there and then
- Be prepared to give it time, but go back to staff about issues raised

Support Options

There are a number of different ways in which staff can seek the kind of support that they may require after a potentially traumatic incident. Incidents are potentially rather than actually traumatic, in the sense that the same incident may stir up all kinds of stress for one person but for another it appears like water rolling off a duck's back. On the other hand, a member of staff who appears not to have been too deeply affected may react strongly at a later stage.

Apart from counselling, some staff can be helped by relaxation (tapes or training), or meditation, such as TM (transcendental meditation), prayer, sport, swimming, running or massage as well as group discussion. It can be very empowering to realise the variety of options that may help, none of them a panacea, but all likely to be better than excessive alcohol or other drugs in helping people recover from a traumatic experience.

Whether staff are 'under the doctor' or not, after an incident, good support avoids over-medicalising the situation. A 'sickness' label can stick and make people feel that they are abnormal or ill, in such a way that recovery may be impaired. The notion of being a 'victim' has similar dangers.

> The staff were very agitated in the open plan finance section, after the husband of one of the staff had killed their youngest child on his second birthday. A counsellor was asked to come in to run some short support sessions for staff in groups of about half a dozen, prior to the baby's mother returning to work. The departmental head told the counsellor that she was particularly concerned about Alec, one of the supervisors and a young father himself who had attempted suicide two months previously after a row with his partner. In the event, Alec told the counsellor that he had just been to hell and back and was not intending to have a return visit and would really concentrate on trying to help the baby's mother and the other staff through the weeks ahead. This is just what he in fact did, amazing the departmental head with his previously unseen maturity and concern for others. One or two other staff, however, took up the option of some short-term support with the counsellor.

Follow-Up by the Line Manager

Some of the follow up may be delegated to a human resources manager, but it is important that the line manager is seen as personally committed to the well-being of the staff. He or she delegates that concern at their peril and needs to find ways of expressing it and checking out how people are from time to time.

If staff are on prescribed medication as a result of the incident, there may be implications for the ability of staff to work accurately and safely. Consultation with occupational health or their GP, with the staff member's permission, may be appropriate before the person returns to full duties or, equally, before changing their job.

Voluntary One-to-One Counselling

Counselling can be helpful (see Chapter 4), but should be seen as optional. On the other hand, the message should also be that it is not a sign of weakness to talk things over with a counsellor. The senior manager on site can set an example by letting the staff know that he or she is having a chat with the counsellor. Staff can be encouraged to have one session as a sort of personal insurance, on the basis that it should do no harm and may be useful.

The counsellors and managers must not collude with each other to exaggerate the benefits of seeing a counsellor as opposed to the support people can receive from each other and their managers. Access to counsellors must not undermine the listening and counselling skills others may have, with or without training. There can be a danger that managers feel unnecessarily deskilled by having a counsellor around. Consequently an important role for the counsellor may be to support, help and affirm the manager in what he or she is trying to do, rather than take over the main support role.

Isobel complained of a pain in her chest and was taken home by the branch manager, Peter. When he got back to the office he mentioned to Isobel's sister Rachel that Isobel hadn't been feeling too well, and he had taken her home. They neither thought more of it, being unaware of the symptoms of a heart attack. When Isobel's husband arrived home that evening he found that she had died during the day. The bereavement for Peter and especially Rachel was full of guilt that they had not followed up, and checked that she was alright during the day. She had given the appearance of being so fit that they had never dreamt that she was about to have a heart attack.

Although Isobel had actually died at home, the company treated it as if she had died at work in terms of the support they offered to the staff with whom she worked. In this instance, the company offered both Rachel and Peter some counselling support, which helped them through some of the worst of it. The counsellor also had one meeting with the two of them, which they found useful, as the shared guilt that they both felt had put a strain on their working relationship. Rachel originally felt that she could not go on working there, but the quality of the support she felt that she received from colleagues, as well as the counsellor, helped change her mind. The company was pleased because she was a valued and trustworthy member of staff.

After a traumatic incident, counselling is often best offered over the first 2 or 3 weeks in the first instance or a brief number of sessions of, say, up to about 10, although some staff will find one or two both useful and enough. If the company has an EAP (Employee Assistance Programme), this would probably be in line with the number of sessions available to all staff with a counsellor. After that, if more counselling seems appropriate, a decision will need to be worked through with the human resources or senior line manager. Is support to be offered with the same counsellor through the company or should the counsellor help the staff member link to a completely external counsellor or agency, such as CRUSE?

A Visit from 'Top' Management

This can be very helpful but can misfire and be counter-productive, depending on the pre-existing reputation and relationship with staff of the top managers concerned but, most of all, on the way they behave when they are there. If they come over as genuinely concerned, human, not on their dignity nor in a cloud of self-importance, the back-up the immediate line manager involved can be tremendous.

Tony had given the impression of being very task centred, not much of a people person after his appointment as the new Division Director. The business was in a precarious state and he put in place a number of initiatives that involved moving some senior managers, a few out of the company. Then the general manager of one of the overseas branches was murdered, and Tony went straight out there, spending time with the traumatised Management Team helping them pick up the pieces and also with the manager's family, making sure that they got the support that they needed. One of the staff said later that they got to see Tony's humanity in a way that they might never have done, but for the tragedy.

A trap for the top manager, distracted by many other pressing demands for his or her attention, can be to appear to be going through the motions, not really engaged at a human level with what has happened. Colin Parry wrote of his disappointment with both John Major, the Prime Minister, and John Smith, the Leader of the Opposition, on their visit to Warrington after the IRA bomb which killed his young son Tim and Johnathan Ball in 1993.

> My disappointment with (them both) stemmed from the fact that neither man asked me anything other than the orthodox and polite question 'How are you?' This question is rarely answered honestly. You know they don't expect a long and detailed reply and so you don't give one. This is the unspoken understanding between the questioner and the person being questioned and is part of the ritual in our polite society.

Colin described the different impact that his local MP, David Alton, and the Irish President, Mary Robinson, made through their ability to convey a genuine wish to hear his views and opinions. They also communicated a greater awareness of what had happened to the Parry family and how they had responded to the tragedy. The difference may have been because of the greater interest of these two in the event, rather than concern for the people affected. John Major, for example, had taken the trouble immediately after Tim's death to write a sensitive and hand written letter to the Parrys, model behaviour for a caring chief executive.[6]

A Chief Executive going to a funeral or making a personal visit must take the trouble to be well briefed beforehand and to have thought about what to say and what to ask if the effort made is to be experienced as helpful. This applies to young people as well. Tim Parry's older brother, for example, was asked endlessly by visiting dignitaries what he wanted to do when he left school, as if they could not find a way of acknowledging his own loss.[7]

Sensitivity is also required of the top manager in relation to the line, human resources and other managers more directly involved. Top management involvement has to aim to reinforce, complement and support, rather than outshine, the others. This has to be subtly interwoven with an alertness to the overall adequacy of the company response to an extremely difficult situation.

The General Stress Reaction

Not all who are close to someone who dies suddenly become overstressed, but anyone may do, irrespective of the strength of character they may be assumed to have. How stressed they become can be in part due to the level of distress they experience at the loss of the person and the circumstances of their death. There may, however, be other factors, possibly unknown to people at work, such as what is going on in their life outside work in terms of loss and pressure. All of these factors (as in the list of Life Change Index in the addendum at the end of this chapter) use up some of our reservoir of psychological and physical energy and resilience. The death of someone at work can stimulate the stress response in what may be for some a real sense of crisis.

The Stress Response

Alarm
stage 1

Fight or flight: the body
and brain prepare for action;
people rally round with energy
or disappear fast!

– speed up
– talk quickly
– move and walk faster
– eat and drink faster

Resistance
stage 2

Fats, sugars and cortico steroids
released for more energy

– irritable
– gastric symptoms
– tension
– insomnia

Exhaustion
stage 3

Energy stores used up

– 'cotton wool' head
– palpitations
– depression
– fatigue

If stress is building up in someone anyway, irrespective of a triggering event, such as a death at work, there are a number of ways in which it emerges: in the way we feel, the way we think, the way we behave and in the way our body reacts. Even though all of these four aspects of stress may be operating within an individual, one of the categories may be more obvious than the others. For example, some people's emotions are near the surface, and it is seldom a mystery how they are feeling. On the other hand, other people keep their feelings hidden from others, even perhaps from themselves and they are easier to know through their thinking. Others keep both their emotions and their thinking well buried most of the time. They are doers but express themselves through their behaviour.

If you are concerned about the level of stress staff may be under, be alert and sensitive to all four aspects of the way that stress finds expression:

Ways in which Stress is Expressed

Feelings	*Thinking*	*Behaviour*	*Bodily Reactions*
Angry	Confused	Drink too much	Constipation
Anxious	Defensive	Eat too much	Diarrhoea
Helpless	Forgetful	Restless	Dizziness
Irritable	Going round	Sleeplessness	Heartburn
Worrying	in circles		Tight jaw
Nervous	Indecisive	Smoke too much	Heart rate
			increase
Miserable	Loss of	Trembling	Hot & cold spells
Tired	concentration		Sweating
Panicky	Nightmares		Legs turn to jelly
Tense			Muscle twitches
Not enjoying			Rapid weight loss
life			or gain

In a crisis, as extra energy is released, people often have enough, even a surplus of, resources, to be able to cope. Support from other people is often forthcoming from work and at home, especially in the short term, until the crisis subsides. As the demands of the crisis continue, the psychological and physical energy may get used up and weariness builds up to the point where the person has nothing left, their ability to work effectively diminishes and collapses.

Taking Care of Yourself

A traumatic event puts demands on your physical, mental and emotional resources, so it is important that you take extra care of yourself afterwards. It is easy to forget or neglect to do this in the midst of all that is going on.

– drink plenty of water, the purer the better.
– eat regular nutritious meals, with plenty of fruit and vegetables.
– ensure that you have regular exercise, as enjoyable as possible, preferably some of it in the fresh air.
– breathe deeply and easily, filling and emptying your lungs fully.
– beware of increasing your intake of coffee, tea, alcoholic drinks, cigarettes, sweets or junk food: preferably cut back to avoid getting more depressed through that avenue.
– be prepared to allow time and opportunity to talk through what happened and its impact on you with those close to you, if they are able and prepared to listen, and/or with someone in a counselling role.
– give yourself the best chance of sleeping well, but if you cannot, be prepared to get up and do something else before trying again.
– relax to reduce muscle tension through some combination, for example, of meditation, swimming, relaxation exercises, walking, soaking in a hot bath and massage.[8]

Life Change Index

The ranking of 43 common experiences on a numerical scale of Life Change Units (LCU), after Thomas H.Holmes & Richard Rahe:

Rank Life Events	LCU Value	Rank	Life Events	LCU Value
1. Death of a partner	100	23.	Son or daughter leaves home	29
2. Divorce	73	24.	In-law trouble	29
3. Separation	65	25.	Outstanding personal achievement	28
4. Spell in jail	63	26.	Partner starts/stops work	26
5. Death of close family member	63	27.	Begin or end school	26
6. Personal injury	53	28.	Change of living conditions	25
7. Marriage	50	29.	Change of personal habits	24
8. Loss of job	47	30.	Trouble with employer	23

9. Marital reconciliation	45	31.	Change in working hours or conditions	20
10. Retirement	45	32.	Change in residence	20
11. Change in health of a family member	44	33.	Change in schools	20
12. Pregnancy	40	34.	Change in recreation	19
13. Sex difficulties	39	35.	Change in church activities	19
14. New family member	39	36.	Change in social activities	19
15. Business merger/ change	39	37.	Smaller mortgage or loan	17
16. Change in personal finances	38	38.	Change in sleeping habits	16
17. Death of close friend	37	39.	Change in number of family get-togethers	15
18. Change to a different type of work	36	40.	Change in eating habits	15
19. Change in number of arguments with partner	35	41.	Holiday	13
20. Having a large mortgage or loan	31	42.	Christmas	12
21. Foreclosure of mortgage or loan	30	43.	Minor violations of the law	11
22. Changes of responsibilities at work	29			

* *Scoring over 300 points in one year is said to increase the risk of becoming ill: 80% probability quoted in the following 2 years.*
* *A score of between 150 and 300 points in one year is said to mean a risk of becoming ill: 51% in the following 2 years.*
* *A score of less than 150 in one year is said to mean a risk of becoming ill: 37% in the following 2 years.*

Source: *Strategies in Self-Awareness*, The Marylebone Health Centre, 17 Marylebone Road, London NW1 5LT, UK

Notes

1. National Center for Post Traumatic Stress Disorder *Clinical Newsletter* 3/1 Winter (NCPTSD, Palo Alto, CA, USA, 1993).

2. File on 4, (BBC Radio 4, 21 February 1999).

3. Ibid.

4. Bergman, David *Deaths at Work – Accidents Or Corporate Crime*: *The Failure Of Inquests and The Criminal Justice System* (The Workers' Educational Association, Temple House, 9 Upper Berkeley Street, London W1H 8BY).

5. Feltham, Colin, editor *The Gains of Listening*: *Perspectives on Counselling at Work* (Open University Press, Buckingham, UK 1997).

6. Parry, Colin & Wendy, *Tim: An Ordinary Boy* (Hodder & Stoughton, 1994).

7. Ibid.

8. Callaghan, Ashley *Relaxation*: *Self Help Exercises An Audio Tape* (CEPEC, London).

Children and Young People

Introduction

The issue of children's bereavement is largely beyond the scope of this book, but this chapter is included for two reasons. Unresolved issues around childhood grief can often impact on us as adults, and may affect how we cope with our lives later on. Secondly, it is easy to ignore or underestimate what children are going through after a death in the family or the death of a friend. Even in a relatively protected country, like the UK, about 1% of children are bereaved of a parent every year, that is about 135,000. It is estimated that 20 babies a day die at or soon after birth and 9000 young people a year die before they reach the age of 14 as a result of illness or accident. Many of these young people have siblings. An excellent book by Sister Frances Dominica, the founder of a children's hospice in Oxford, is aptly subtitled 'helping parents to do things their way when their child dies'.[1] That is an important principle of support for the grieving of any age.

Adults can easily feel confused about the grief of children, as if they inhabit a different emotional universe. What it was like to be a child can be quickly forgotten in the mists of time. What is more they may have had no significant experience of grief, when they were young themselves. Children, like their elders, are individuals and personalities vary. Parents may see similarities in their own and their son or daughter's personality, but they quickly need to learn that they are not clones and '... have their own thoughts.'

It is understandable that people want to protect a child, as far as possible, from the pain of grief . They may also not want to intrude inappropriately on their grief and do or say the wrong thing. Avoidance can become a tempting strategy. The understanding of children about death can also be underestimated in order to protect the adults from being exposed to how they really feel. Furthermore if those nearest to the child are themselves grieving, they may feel their emotional reserves are running dry and they have nothing left for the children.

The age when children are old enough to grieve continues to be a topic for debate. William Worden,[2] from his experience, including a study of 70 American grieving families and their children, concluded that children can mourn normally by the age of 3 or 4, although others have argued that this capacity is not developed until adolescence. Dr Naomi Richman, a child psychiatrist who has worked with children coping with war and violence, has observed that there is evidence that children too young to speak are affected by witnessing violence: images can be remembered even at 18 months.[3] Pioneering work in supporting children who have witnessed such terrible crimes as the murder of their mother by their father has been undertaken by Dr Dora Black of the Royal Free Hospital in London. She uses a 'witness to violence' interview, similar to the debriefing interview for survivors of disasters. The drawings of children exposed to terrible experiences of violence leave no doubt as to the impact of that violence on them.[4,5]

John Bowlby argued that infants, coming to terms with the process of separation, experience grief reactions as young as six months. His studies included infants in hospital, at a time when it was common for parents to be kept away, even from visiting. The idea was that the appearance and departure of parents upset them, because they cried powerfully. Keep mothers, especially, away and the children stopped crying, often becoming listless and depressed although superficially easier for the staff to manage. Bowlby's work was influential in helping to change this practice to one of encouraging frequent and longer visits. Where possible, for very young children, a parent often now stays with them virtually all the time while they are in hospital. He demon-

strated how deeply children can grieve at the loss, albeit temporary, of the people on whom they most depend.[6]

There are many factors that bear down in different ways on
children and young people, as on adults, influencing the impact
of a close bereavement. These are clues to the child who may
need extra support to help them pull through:

The death itself
If it was sudden and/or violent or even if it was unexpected for the
child, because he or she was not prepared for it, that is likely to
make the grieving even more difficult than it might have been
anyway.

The person who has died
If the deceased was the mainstay of their security – especially if he
or she was a single parent.
If the child disliked or felt jealous of the bereaved.
If the child cannot speak of the person or idealises them or feels
particularly guilty,
Any of these factors are likely to make the grieving more difficult.

The surviving parent(s)
If they lack support, are unemployed, have serious health difficulties of their own or are depressed, withdrawn, preoccupied with
themselves to the detriment of their children or are finding it difficult to cope (as opposed to grieving strongly) that is also a source
of added pressure on the child.

The family
The immediate or extended family, instead of being a resource,
may in some cases be a source of further difficulty, with tensions,
undue conflict or demanding siblings, especially the very young.

The child himself or herself
Irrespective of the above the child will be helped in their ability to
cope with their loss if they are blessed with self confidence, a sense
of being respected, admired and loved for themselves rather than
their achievements or strength, ideally both from their family and
peer group.

Children's Grief

How children grieve will be strongly influenced by their stage of
emotional development. Adults supporting children should,
therefore, be even more careful not to make assumptions about
what they may be feeling than they would with adults. That is
particularly important if the adult is a parent or someone else
very close to the child, who may be more tempted to think that

they know what the child is going through. Listening sensitively, but not too intrusively, to pick up clues in the child's behaviour as well as what he or she says is crucial in providing support.

Young children are naturally very egotistical and feel that they are the centre of their world. Part of growing up is to become increasingly aware that this is not the case and that they do not have control or responsibility for all that goes on around them. This egotism impacts on their grieving process, in that it is not uncommon for them to be burdened by an unreasonable strand of guilt if a parent, sibling or someone else very close to them dies or is killed. They can feel personally responsible for all kinds of reasons. They had a row with the deceased, they did not love them well enough or they are being punished with their death for some reason. That reason may not be directly to do with the person who has died at all: for example, they may have been misbehaving or thinking hateful thoughts about someone. In supporting children, others need to be alert to this possibility of some such guilt, which can be directly addressed.

School

School is the workplace for many children, with similar issues facing teachers as managers. They also have to strive for the balance between crowding or intruding upon a bereaved child or one with a terminally ill parent or sibling and, on the other hand, failing to acknowledge the loss. In one fifth form, a girl suddenly started to cry. Her father had died two years earlier and she said that when she came back, nobody in the school mentioned it. It is important that the child is reassured sensitively that the opportunity is available for them to talk to someone they trust, whether that is a member of staff and/or a friend.

With young children, in particular, there are three common strategies adopted by responsible adults: distraction, ignoring and empathy. Many teachers still seem only to have the first two in their repertoire and find it hard to distinguish between a child who is mildly upset or dramatising their feelings and one who is really upset and for whom some active listening, respect for them and empathy is needed. Distraction and ignoring are fine options sometimes to be used sparingly, but not when they are used invariably or unthinkingly.

Before a pupil returns after the death of a family member, their teacher can sometimes usefully talk with the class about how they might feel returning to school in those circumstances, preparing to get the balance as right as possible between a continual stream of sympathy and ignoring them completely. Anecdotal evidence suggests that the latter is the more common problem, as the culture of denial is so strong in many schools. Peer conformity is also an inevitable factor among young people, and to be bereaved is not conforming to most norms in British schools. Where there is a more public tragedy and the culture affirms mourning, children can be remarkably able in both grieving at school and also in supporting each other. Nevertheless, teachers need to be vigilant for signs that the vulnerability of bereavement does not becomes a magnet for bullying.

Saying Goodbye

If a parent is terminally ill, they may want to write letters or notes or put together a scrap book for the child or children they are to leave behind. As inadequate as these inevitably feel and as heart breaking to do, they can be treasured later. Children and parent may want to think about what kind of things they want to say to each other: expressing their appreciation and love, forgiveness for the quarrels or fights they have had, or asking each other questions, before it is too late, that they have been meaning to ask but have not got round to asking. If that opportunity is missed it can be a source of great and ongoing painful regret afterwards. Sometimes they can be supported to create that opportunity, rather than forlornly hoping it will just happen.

When it is a child who is dying, Claudia Jewett expressed the experience of many when she wrote:

> Even when children have an intuitive sense of their own impending death, they may be reluctant or afraid to bring it up because they don't want to upset their parents. And so the child faces the unknown, anxious and alone. Both caregivers and child wait for the other to indicate a readiness to talk about what is happening, When the topic does come up, it is not unusual for the dying child to be visibly relieved to have permission finally to ask questions and to receive the parents' reassurances and support.[7]

The Meaning of Death

Death has different meanings for children, as it does for adults (see chapter 11), depending on their culture and beliefs and the beliefs of those around them. At first the idea that the dead person exists somewhere else makes some sense to the child, hence the importance of the idea of heaven as a physical reality. Before Copernicus and his followers made such a concept incredible for most people, religious and irreligious, there was the possibility of the adult view of death in many countries equating with that of the child. In general, separation for young children is the primary pain, whereas the finality of death may dawn on them slowly to the point, perhaps at the age of 10 or 11 when they may come to realise that death is both inevitable and inescapable for us all.

The meaning of death also depends for children on its familiarity. In many developed countries in Europe and North America, for example, modern medicine and the death taboo mean that children have little contact with the dying or are likely to see dead bodies. Furthermore some of the basic facts can be kept from them in such a way that, if they discover them for themselves, can be the more frightening.

In most developing countries or indeed places where there are wars or natural disasters, it is likely to be very different for children. They are likely to see dead bodies at an early age. In such circumstances, illusions about what happens to a body after death do not last long. The mystery and questions about what happens – if anything – to the person's spirit, of course, remain.

When Sarah was 13, she had a row with her mother at breakfast. They did not part on good terms. Tragically, her mother was injured in an accident on the way from work. Sarah was told of the accident by a friend of the family, but given no opportunity to visit her mother in hospital. Her father was in the hospital most of the time, but seemed to avoid her when he did come home. A week later, the same friend told Sarah that her mother had died, but her father never did get round to talking with her about it. She was also not given the opportunity to attend the funeral. 10 years later, a personal crisis catapulted her into a need to talk through how she still felt about the tragedy. She felt that her partner's stiff upper lip mirrored her father's failure to give her any support at the time she most needed it and him. She retained a sense that men in her life failed to be concerned about how she really felt about painful issues. Her partner caught some of the unresolved sense of her anger towards her father, an important complicating factor when they unravelled the communication issues between the two of them in the present.

Young People and Mourning

When children are excluded from the mourning process, some adults like Sarah carry with them unresolved grief from childhood, which reinforces the intensity of their experience of loss later in life. To make matters worse, a child is sometimes made to feel, especially if they have reached adolescence, that their loss of a parent is secondary to the surviving parent's loss of a spouse. They may be expected to support the latter and deny their own loss, especially if everybody else seems to be doing so around them.

While teenagers, especially boys, may be expected to be strong for others in the family, their own bereavement is hardly acknowledged. The idea may be floating under the surface that young people have had most of the crucial parenting by the time they hit the teens. Now they can appear closer to their peer group and are looking away from the family for the focus of their life. Their loss can be underestimated, even by them. Good parental support is central to a good transition into adult life. The teenager who loses a parent is losing the chance of sharing with him or her all the triumphs, experiences, milestones, difficulties and crises in the rest of their life.

If children have not reached adolescence, their grief may be ignored for a different reason. They are, perhaps, thought to be too young to be upset by bereavement except by mentioning it. Then they may be pitched by later events or unexpectedly into grief as an adult for someone they lost as a child.

A surviving parent needs to go through their own mourning but also to find ways of sharing some of that with their children. Giving children the attention that they need at this time may be difficult but it is essential that they do receive it. If possible it is important that it comes to a considerable degree from a surviving parent. The quality of extended 'family' or community support is important, from grandparents, aunts and uncles, neighbours or work colleagues, whoever is near and close.

When Ian's wife died leaving him with a 6-year-old son, elderly neighbours took on an unofficial grandparenting role and became a rock of care for the boy, constantly playing with him and giving him tea, when he came home from school. Though there was no flexitime system at Ian's work, that did not stop his manager, Angus, suggesting to Ian that he come in late two or three days a week so that he could take his son to school. Angus had made the suggestion, because he touched base regularly with Ian enough to know 'how it was going'.

This checking out was focused and did not take a great deal of time, maybe half an hour a week on average. Angus was in no doubt that that time was part of his managerial responsibilities, not an optional extra because he had a kind heart. At a time like this especially, Angus wanted Ian to be as successful a salesman as possible, but not at the expense of being a good father. He knew that Ian's enthusiasm and motivation would only be undermined if he was worried more than necessary about his son's welfare. Ian was largely free of divided loyalties, because of the level of support that he received from the workplace.

Whether loss is acknowledged for young people may depend on the formality of the relationship. A parent's death can be seen as very sad, while they may be expected to take that of an aunt or uncle in their stride, irrespective of how close the person may have been. Aunts, uncles, cousins and many other members of the extended family can be remote or close to the young person, whose grieving may vary accordingly. At times, such hierarchies are institutionalised for young people as well as people at work. So, for example, in a British young offenders unit, the inmates may be allowed to attend the funeral of a parent or sibling, but not a grandparent. In some cases however the inadequacy of the relationship with their parents may be a contributing factor to them being inside. Grandparents can be the adults to whom they feel closest. In one such unit, Onley near Rugby, an imaginative chaplain offered a service in the chapel at the same time as the funeral, when such a grandparent could be remembered and honoured.

Daniel was the industrial relations manager in the motor industry, whose story was described more fully in chapter 4. After his father had left, he had lived with his younger sister and his mother, who when Daniel was 13 had collapsed in front of him, was rushed into hospital (after he alerted a neighbour) and died a week later. A few hours after her death, he was summoned to the hospital. There he was told by a priest, whom he did not know, that she had died. Daniel was then directed by the priest to kiss her and to go and tell his younger brother this terrifying news. Neither the priest nor anyone else apparently enabled him to talk about what was going on, to ask questions or to say how he felt. Like so many children in this situation, Daniel was locked into isolation by the insensitivity of the adult world. He was told to kiss his mother without warning or an explanation of how cold her body would be.

When we die, our body normally becomes naturally cold within an hour or so, but Daniel was experiencing the unnatural cold of a refrigerated body, which can shock people of any age if they are not prepared for it. We experience each other through all our senses, but touch is especially important in intimate relationships, such as that of a mother and child. It is especially important that children are warned gently that the dead body of a parent may feel and smell as well as look different to the very familiar person she was when alive. The fact that some of the feelings and smells are artificial to prevent decomposition is an added complication to the experience of being with the body of someone who has died.

Viewing the Body and the Funeral

For children, seeing the body can help them understand some of the reality of death, although care needs to be taken in case the person appears to look odd, and some explanation may be needed. Sensitivity is needed in explaining what the person looks like. Sometimes the body is made up to look even more unnatural than if they had been left more or less alone. I was with my mother when she died, and after a few minutes I drove to my sister's home to collect my family to come and pay their respects. It took me an hour or so, but when we got back, my mother's jaw had not been closed and had in death dropped open, making her look somewhat peculiar. My young boys were in no way put out, however, and took it all in their stride, one asking 'I wonder what Grandma was saying when she died'.

Children are often mistakenly kept away from the funeral and feel it keenly later, although attitudes may be changing. When Virginia Ironside focused on the question 'Can a small child cope with a funeral?' in her column in the *Times* newspaper, 'scores of readers wrote in, many still smarting from being denied the chance when they were young to attend the funeral of a much-loved relative'. One of them, William Mathieson, who grew up in Liverpool in the '20s and '30s when the mortality rate among children was high, said that then 'it was common practice to lay out the bodies of children and adults in the front parlour. The front door of the house was left open and children and neighbours were free to go in at any time to view the corpse. I cannot recall any child being upset by this practice'.[8]

The purposes of the funeral (see chapter 15) do not only apply to adults. At the very least children should be given good information about the purpose of the funeral and what will take place, before being given the choice of whether to attend or not. In the case of a funeral of a parent or sibling, even though attending may feel like an ordeal, being left out of it may be worse, especially in the longer run. Being at (or even taking a part in) the funeral is a way of the importance of their relationship with the deceased being recognised and for them to honour him or her and continue the process of acknowledging that they have died. It also can give them a sense that others also cared about the one they loved.

The child's flowers or wreath should be given prominence on the coffin. They may also want to include symbolically a note, a drawing or memento in the coffin. It is important to ensure that their understanding that the person is no longer in the body is reinforced before and perhaps also at the funeral before it disappears for cremation or is lowered into the ground for burial.

In William Worden's study[9] of 125 bereaved American children, between the ages of 6 and 17, 95% of them attended the funeral. In most families there was very little discussion about whether or not to include the children in this ritual. It was generally assumed that they would be there and they were. Children were included in the funeral planning and in the funeral itself in various ways. Being included also helped children to feel important and useful when many were feeling overwhelmed. A 10 year old boy who helped carry his father's coffin said: 'It was kinda heavy but it felt good to carry his coffin'.

Generally it was a positive experience, but the quality of preparation of the children for the funeral was important.

Some people are helped by preparing for the death of someone close to them while they are dying, but children, especially younger ones, are less likely to be aware of terminal illness than adults, unless they are informed sensitively about what is going on. If that does not happen, they can be very bitter that they were not given the opportunity of saying their goodbyes, asking questions of the person while it was still possible or even just saying how much they loved the person.

Children of a Parent who Has Committed Suicide

It is difficult to reassure a child easily that they are not to blame and that the person did not want to leave them, in the case of suicide. The child will need to explore the reasons for such a drastic act, and their own feelings about it. They may feel guilty, sad, frightened and angry with the parent. If they think of the parent as unhinged mentally that can reinforce the fear that they may one day take the same path.

If they regard them as sane, they may feel desolate at the apparent lack of care or love that allowed them to an act in a way in which their own needs were so apparently disregarded. Even if the person was seriously or terminally ill, such feelings may surface on the basis that they were robbed of a few days, weeks, months or years of their company.

Where suicide was triggered by despair or acute depression, at some stage they may need to think through the alternative options that their parent did not take, on the basis that other such options will be available to them later in life. Suicide is unlikely to be their only choice in the face of adversity. They will not have to follow in their footsteps on this one.

When Alex was 12, his father committed suicide, leaving him feeling stricken, guilty and bewildered. As the only son, he felt that if his relationship with his father had been better, it would not have happened. There was no note left and he had to cope with his transition into manhood without a close male role model nor a father with whom to talk things over. His mother seemed too distraught to take an interest in him or listen to how he felt. Alex ploughed a very lonely furrow for the next 10 years. After that his life took on a new direction: marriage, his own family and a good job following academic success at university. When he was made redundant in his thirties, however, after a successful career for 15 years, Alex had a crisis in confidence in which all the questions around his father's death resurfaced, as if it had happened only recently. The job search needed to be postponed for a while until he had worked through and recovered from some of the grief that had been 'on hold'.

Supporting Each Other

There is a number of local initiatives, such as support groups, organised by different agencies, to help young people support each other. One project, for example, initiated a newsletter for bereaved teenagers. In one issue, Rachel, aged 14, wrote of her experience of living with her mother's cancer since she was 10:

My mum is still alive at the moment, although nobody knows for how long – two months or two years. Even the doctors don't know. I was given four pieces of advice: – 1. keep your chin up; 2. don't bottle things up; 3. it's nobody's fault; and the most important 4. live life to the full, every day is a new experience.

Lulu, 16, wrote of her mother's death 3 years before:

I can't imagine her being dead. I don't really believe in heaven, so where is she? I can't understand how a person who was here so very alive can now be nowhere. I know we all die some day and death is reality – but I can't envisage it. I miss her each day, because as time goes on it's longer since I last saw her, last spoke to her in the flesh. I miss her to the point that sometimes I think I am going crazy needing to tell her all the things I never told her when she was here. Maybe I just never believed something like this would ever happen.

An 18 year old on the death of his father two years before:

I feel like his death is partly my fault, and that I never got the chance to know him because I don't really talk and my dad wasn't a talker either. I know that I am going to miss him doing father-son things in future because my dad was always there when I wanted him .... I still cry, but I try not to in front of my mum, who is going through hell at the minute, and I try to be strong for her.

One teenager wrote of her thoughts from her mother's perspective shortly after the latter had died:

I don't mind.
I was never like the rest of you,
Making plans about the
Great things I'd do.
I never thought of myself as much.
You were the ones going ahead,
Always, always running off without me.
Now I am the one going ahead – to heaven,
I am not afraid.
If God wants me with him
Then who am I to know better?

Helping Bereaved Children: A Checklist

- listen and notice carefully with your eyes as well as ears.
- be even more sensitive about timing than with adults.
- let them be distracted, get on with their life the way they want to or be in denial.
- offer to talk and provide full and clear information.
- be prepared not to push the child or yourself.
- be alert to and willing to address their fears and anxieties.
- acknowledge and respect the child's feelings.
- reassure them that they will be cared for.
- be alert to the fear that the remaining parent or they will die.
- maintain consistency of care, not inappropriate lax discipline.
- be prepared to reassure them that they are not to blame.
    - And that the person did not want to leave them
    - And that they will not return, at least in this life.
- discuss the death and the person sensitively, naturally and openly so that the children can do the same, when they want to.
- give the child time and opportunity to remember the dead person before being encouraged to sever bonds a little in order to get on with their life.
- be honest, not least about your own beliefs about an after-life.
- do not be afraid to show some of your own feelings, including tears, in front of the child: it may make them feel less disturbed about their own.
- do not minimise their sadness over the death of a pet.
- be careful about praising them for being brave or pressurising them to be brave and not to express how they really feel.
- help them express how they feel in different ways about the person, death and/or their death, for example, through drawings, sculpting in clay, poetry and other writing and other forms of play.
- write letters to the deceased in the present tense, but be careful.
- help them, if they want, to produce a scrapbook of memories, using drawings, pictures, press cuttings, photos and their own and perhaps others' writings.
- create and notice opportunities to remember and celebrate the person who has died, such as birthdays and other anniversaries, so their memory is not buried and forgotten.
- be prepared for them to need some bereavement counselling or other external support, especially but not exclusively within the first two years.

Notes

1. Dominica, Sister Frances *Just My Reflection*: *helping parents to do things their way when their child dies* (DLT, London, 1997).

2. Worden, W. *Children and Grief* (Guildford Press, New York and London, 1996).

3. Ibid.

4. Black, Dora and others *Father Kills Mother*: *Post-Traumatic Stress Disorder in the Children* (Bereavement Care: Cruse, London, Spring 1993).

5. Gill, Liz 'Growing up after Tragedy' (*The Times*, London, 18th August 1992).

6. Bowlby, J. *Attachment and Loss*: *Loss, Sadness and Depression* (Basic Books, New York, 1980).

7. Jewett, Claudia, *Helping Children Cope with Separation and Loss*: *Childcare Policy and Practice* (B.T. Batsford, London, 1982).

8. Ironside, Virginia, *Times*, 1992.

9. Worden, W. *Children and Grief*, (Guildford Press, New York and London, 1996).

Further Resources

The Child Bereavement Trust, launched in 1994, Brindley House, 4 Burkes Road, Beaconsfield, Bucks HP9 1PB, telephone: 01494 678 088.

Winston's Wish: A Grief Support Programme for Children, founded in 1992. Gloucestershire Hopsital, Great Western Road, Gloucester GL1 3NN, telephone: 01452 394 377.

10

The Practical Tasks after Death

- Selecting an Undertaker or Funeral Director
- Registering the death
- Funeral Arrangements
- The Will
- Letters of Sympathy
- State benefits
- Children
- Throwing Things Away

Selecting an Undertaker or Funeral Director

Be as clear as possible what you want before you approach an undertaker. For example, Nancy and Gordon wanted the body of their young son to stay at home after his death until the funeral, except for being taken away to be embalmed. They rang around half a dozen undertakers in the town, only one of which was prepared to accommodate the heartfelt wishes of their family on this point. The telephoning may be done by a friend on behalf of the next-of-kin, which may make negotiating on various points, including money, more bearable for them.

Be careful that in the heightened emotion of immediate bereavement you do not select the most expensive coffin and cars to go the funeral, unless that is really what is wanted and afford-able. Most undertakers will also advise on an inexpensive and simple coffin, possibly including the biodegradable option of cardboard.

Good funeral directors will concentrate primarily on what your wishes and needs are and help you clarify them, while also giving you the information you want and perhaps need. In other words they will be more marketing than sales orientated. There are still some inadequate undertakers, however, who will be ineffective listeners and tell you what you should do, because they are the experts. When you do meet them, do not rush into a decision that you may later regret, but take what they have said into account, and be prepared to tell them you will telephone or contact them in an hour or two, when you have had a chance to think it over.

Registering the Death

Once a doctor has certified that the person is dead, he or she will give the next-of-kin or the closest member of the family available a death certificate. If the person is to be cremated, two certificates signed by different doctors will be needed. Normally the death should be registered within five days (or eight in Scotland) with the Registry of Births, Deaths and Marriages. After cremation, there is no way the body can be exhumed if suspicion arises about the manner of the person's death.

Whoever goes to the Registry Office needs to take details of the birth place and date, a note from the doctor and, if signed, the certificate of death. The Registrar will provide the certificate that allows the funeral to go ahead, for the funeral director. A copy will also be needed to claim any social security money, for which the next-of-kin may be eligible, and, if appropriate, a widow's pension. A third copy may be useful for claiming life insurance payments. It is often worth getting three or four copies of the certificate for such purposes as these.

Funeral Arrangements

These are more fully discussed in chapter 15, but be sure to negotiate the kind of funeral that is most appropriate for the person who has died, bearing in mind their wishes and those of the next-of-kin and close family.

Flowers or Donations?

Some people want to do something tangible and giving flowers is the traditional way of doing this. Think about whether this is what you want and, if it is, what you would like to do with any flowers collected at the church or crematorium. They can be just left there, or taken home or given to a hospital, church or somewhere else where they will be appreciated. Alternatively people can be asked to contribute to a favourite charity or other cause close to the heart of the person who has died. Once you have decided, make sure that you communicate your wishes to and through other people.

Letting People Know

This is a time consuming task, and while some next-of-kin want to do some, if not all, of it, this is a job that can be organised for them, if that is their wish. Care should be taken in reaching precise agreement about the message. Some or all of the following might or might not be included:

- cause, time and place of death;
- was it expected or unexpected;
- health of the deceased before he or she died;
- who is the next-of-kin;
- date, time and place of the funeral, and who is welcome;
- flowers or donation to a charity;
- whether the next-of-kin would welcome contact.

Apart from family and friends, others who may need to be considered include:

1) Children's school or college
2) Employer, close colleagues, customers and other business contacts
3) Trade union or professional association
4) The employer of the next-of-kin
5) Deceased's place of worship
6) Other organisations with which he or she was closely involved
7) Landlord
8) Department of Social Security
9) Executor(s) of the will
10) Accountant/solicitor/bank/insurance company
11) Provider of any mortgage, loan, hire purchase agreement, credit cards

The Will

If there is no will, an application needs to be made for 'Letters of Administration' from the Probate Registry (or the local Sheriff's Court in Scotland for confirmation).

Letters of Sympathy

Decide whether they are to be answered and whether they are to be kept. It is easy to lose things when in distress. It can be helpful to ask the bereaved person where they would like to keep the letters, and maybe even to help put them there. Later, they can be read through and perhaps acknowledged by a standard card or letter, with some space for a hand written message, unless the person really wants to answer each one individually.

State Benefits

If social security grants have been claimed, it is necessary to visit, write or telephone the local Benefits Agency (Department of Social Security), or it may be possible for someone from the office to call on the next-of-kin. The address is in the telephone book. It can be helpful to have someone with you to provide moral support on such a visit.

Children

Discuss with children what they want to do, having first explained the situation to them, and support them, whether it is going to see the body, attending the funeral or undertaking a reading at the funeral. They may follow the adult lead or not, but allow them to participate in the grieving. Respect their loss and their need to grieve in their own way and in their own time, but also see chapter 9.

Throwing Things Away

Be careful not to throw documents or financial records away until the financial matters associated with the person's death have all been resolved. Take your own time to give or to throw away the possessions and clothes of the deceased that you do not want to keep for yourself. This activity needs to be undertaken, but not in a hurry or thoughtlessly, and not necessarily alone. It is an important part of working through the reality of the loss and it can be a real help to have someone with you to provide you with support.

Notes

1. Nuttall, Derek *The Early Days of Grieving* (Beaconsfield Publishers, Beaconsfield, England 1991).

11

What is Death and what Does It Mean?

- Death and Modern Society
- Diversity of Beliefs
- What Happens when We Die?
- Some Personal Thoughts about the Meaning of Death

In contrast with our forebears and much of the developing world, many of us in richer countries live well into adulthood before death intrudes into our lives. Although we share with other creatures the fact that we die, the imagination, which is apparently unique to our species, enables us to envisage death as well as life: our dreams, visions, hopes, fears, anxieties and plans can both be based on the fact that we will die and also the fantasy that we won't.

But we can also live fully in the present. The experience of being alive – both pleasure and pain – can so concentrate our energy and attention on the present moment that it can feel as if death is something which happens only to other people.

> What matters?
> Very little, only ....
> > the flicker of light   within the darkness,
> > the feeling of warmth   within the cold,
> > the knowledge of love   within the void.
> > (remembered by Kay Walker from her childhood)

Death itself can be thought of as both a passive and an active force. The figure of Death in mythology is sometimes given an active character: in Ingmar Bergman's medieval film *The Seventh Seal*, for example, the figure of Death challenges the knight to play chess as a means of postponing the knight's own death. When the game is over, inevitably Death wins, taking the knight's life as the prize. Death is prepared to cheat but always wins in the end. The chess game is a powerful metaphor for millions of different battles with Death. Some of us endeavour to keep Death at bay by building up our health, giving up smoking, saying our prayers or making some sacrifice in order to benefit others. Death can be given many names in this active role, sometimes neutral, as in *The Seventh Seal*, sometimes as a malign force, with such negative names as Satan or the Devil, or the positive personality of an active God who chooses when each of us is to die: 'this night thy soul is required of thee'.

Death can also feel as if it is passive. It has been described as a fact rather than as an experience.[1] It just happens, perhaps by chance: why that night for the heart attack, that journey for the fatal accident? Death can occur without apparent reason. Just as the sun rises on the just and the unjust, so also some people live comfortably to an old age, while others die young.

Death and Modern Society

Our Victorian forebears were much closer to death than we are as part of ordinary life. Advances in environmental health and medicine suggest that it will take longer before death makes its claim on most of us. The time is fast approaching when one in five will be a pensioner and a tenth of our population over 75 years old. With this modern perspective, what we think death means, or does not mean, will have an influence on how we grieve. Not that we should exaggerate the impact of belief on bereavement. The most optimistic views of a wonderful and certain life to come or a conviction that death is the end for us as individuals is only one factor. The pain of the loss is as real for the one person as for the other. Indeed a sure hope of a life after death can even be counter-productive, if handled insensitively, pushing a person to deny and bury their grief. In our own time, it is particularly dangerous to make assumptions on what death may mean to anyone, because we do not have such strong or clear communal beliefs as were formerly widespread. François Mitterand, the late French President, expressed this when he wrote in a foreword to a powerful book about caring for the dying:[2]

How do we learn to die? We live in a world that panics at this question and turns away. Other civilisations before ours looked squarely at death. They mapped the passage for both the community and the individual. They infused the fulfilment of destiny with a richness of meaning. Never perhaps have our relationships with death been as barren as they are in this modern spiritual desert, in which our rush to a mere existence carries us past all sense of mystery. We do not know that we are parching the essence of life of one of its wellsprings.

That assessment rings bells with many in western societies, even though the work of the hospice movement, initiated in Britain by Dame Cicely Saunders, has been part of a contemporary response to death. In hospice care death is respected and the care of the dying considered to be as important as curing those for whom there is the possibility of recovery. In the end, of course, there is no cure for that remarkable condition everyone experiences: life. At some stage, it is invariably fatal! The whole of the evolutionary process depends on life forms, that are born, dying to make space for newcomers, who have the opportunity of being a little different as a consequence. This is not just a biological but also a personal phenomenon. As we grow older, newcomers come into our lives and families, giving us a little less time and resource for the existing needy ones in our community. It is an increasingly challenging issue for people in the present time, with such a dramatically increasing human population and the increasing proportion of vulnerable old and very young in it.

Although we are now repeatedly exposed to images of war and violent death in the media, this may, paradoxically, dull our sensitivity to real death through the distancing effect of film and photograph. Violent death and killing have been prominent themes in entertainment, high and low brow, for a long time. The idea of catharsis suggests that we can get rid of troublesome emotions by expressing or experiencing them through drama, art, the Cup Final, etc. Vicariously involved with others, we are plunged into pity, terror or bloodthirstiness, or a combination of all three. Greek tragedy and Shakespeare remind us that what is offered through the media is not new. But does repeated exposure to images of violent death help us come to terms with the reality of death? A preoccupation with exciting or tragic images of violent death through the media may on the one hand help us come to terms with our fear of it, while on the other sustain and feed that fear. What it often fails to do, however, is help us come to terms realistically with the probability that we will die, albeit in a less dramatic way than in many movies.

Most of us do not die in battle or a shoot-out but routinely in hospital or other institutions, from cardio-vascular diseases, respiratory illnesses or cancer. Nevertheless, when someone we know does die violently it still has a profound effect upon us. Being killed in a crash on the way home from the office on a foggy November evening may lack the false glamour of some screen killings, but it presents those who mourn with the same sense of shock at sudden and totally unexpected death.

> It was just another Monday morning as the Health Trust HR Department cranked into action. It started as usual with the early regular arrivals making some coffee. They remarked that Jean, one of the longest serving members, had not come in yet. Then Malcolm arrived with the news that she had been killed the previous day in a gliding accident. The shock of that news traumatised the whole working group for quite a time. She had been young, healthy and full of life. An empty desk, normally such a mundane phenomenon, became suffused with an aura of sadness. Like a bolt out of the blue, death touched everyone in the department, reminding them of their vulnerability.

Diversity of Beliefs

How bereavement works out in practice will vary from individual to individual, depending on their personality, life experience and beliefs. In the past, within societies, there was a more homogeneous approach to the meaning attached to dying and death. Now we realise that it has different meanings for different people. This is not new, except that in our multicultural post-Darwinian times, the diversity of religious and irreligious belief within societies and often within families is increasing. This sense of diversity affects us in many aspects of our lives. The songwriter Paul Simon expressed it, for example, when he wrote:

> Cultures and artistic movements influence each other by osmosis. The proximity of different cultures, magnified by the speed of technology, offers an irresistible challenge to artists to rearrange languages musically, visually and verbally. Cross-cultural dialogue is inevitable as generations, philosophies and artistic movements bang against each other, intermingle, intermarry and interface. There are many versions of the same truth.[3]

In this chapter, we consequently explore some personal ways of looking at the meaning of death, which reflect some of this diversity of beliefs, religious, humanist, atheist or agnostic, new age and old age. Much of human history has involved societies in which the dominant belief systems, political and religious, have been defined by those with the most power and imposed, sometimes brutally, on the rest. In some parts of the world, the 20th century has seen massive change for at least three reasons. They can be summarised as the rise of democracy as an idea and a system and the realisation, through science, theology and linguistics, that religions and the way people think are evolving and subject to change. Thirdly, travel, migration and communication have increased the experience and knowledge of different cultures and belief systems.

In the contemporary multicultural society, as people take seriously the variety of religions in the world, working out what they really believe can become part of the spiritual journey for many people. Thinking for myself has always been what brings diversity in the first place. Individuals, endeavouring to love truth or God 'with all their mind', as Jesus suggested to his followers, through history have found themselves questioning and challenging the dominant religious or philosophical position taken within their country or society. This questioning has led to the formation of splinter or separate religious groups. Thus Sikhism grew out of Hinduism, Lutheranism out of the Catholic Church of Rome and atheist Stalinism out of the Orthodox Christianity of Czarist Russia.

Today we feel much freer than our forebears to think 'the unthinkable' and to express our beliefs without fear of persecution, although Glen Hoddle might disagree after being sacked as England football manager in 1999, at least in part for expressing a politically incorrect version of his belief in reincarnation. His interview with a journalist illustrated an interesting perspective on belief. Confusion was caused because Hoddle claimed to be a Christian and also to believe in a form of reincarnation. Belief is commonly used to describe a package of ideas and practices to which you are expected to assent if you own a particular label. Hindus, Buddhist and others, especially if their religion originated in Asia, can believe in reincarnation, but not Christians, Jews or Muslims. For them it's the life after death, but not in this universe, or nothing! In practice some Christians do believe in reincarnation.[4]

Belief, however, has a personal as well as a communal meaning. As individuals think and meditate about the mystery of life and death, and open themselves to different experiences, thinkers and ideas, they may as individuals end up believing all kind of things. During their life journey, their beliefs may change over time, without them necessarily jumping religious ship and disowning their main religious or non-religious allegiance. On the other hand, there are many who get on with other aspects of their lives, without particularly bothering about religious issues. They are content to allow their religion or irreligion to provide them with a set of beliefs, which they accept and which resolves some of the uncertainty of 'not knowing what to believe'. Such a view may be linked to a respect for authority or the experts, who are taken to know more about a particular subject than I do, because they specialise in it.

What Happens When We Die?

What happens when we die is for most people a mystery. We do not know, but we have some ideas and perhaps some beliefs and hopes.

> Feare not the grave; assure yourselves
>   With Christ your guide to rise,
> Who shall prepare your princely seats;
>   Your light, your life, your crown
> Is he; rewarding all his saints with glory
> And renown.[5]

A traditional expression of the Christian belief in a personal God and personal survival after death is expressed in the well-known prayer:

We see, to give them back to Thee O God, who gavest them to us. Yet, as thou didst not lose them in giving, so do we not lose them by their return. Not as the world giveth, givest Thou, O Lover of souls. What Thou givest Thou takest not away, for what is Thine is ours also if we are Thine. And life is eternal and love is immortal, and death is only an horizon, and an horizon is nothing save the limit of our sight. Lift us up, strong Son of God, that we may see further; cleanse our eyes that we may see more clearly; draw us closer to Thyself that we may know ourselves to be nearer to our loved ones who are with Thee. And while Thou dost prepare a place for us, prepare us also for that happy place, that where Thou art we may be also for evermore. Amen.

That kind of certainty may have sometimes been as much an expression of hope as faith, a need to believe. The sense that death provided an essential element of justice was also a corner-stone of the efforts in many societies to promote good behaviour. If people seemed to get away with wickedness and crime in this life, their misdemeanours would catch up with them when they died and had to face the ultimate judgement of God, who knew all the evidence. The wool could not be pulled over his eyes by an artful defence! Such faith is still widespread, but it is also being more widely questioned in the modern or post-modern world than in previous centuries.

An example of the varied ways in which belief can be an indi-vidual expression, though influenced by a religious affiliation, is a poem by Simon Burne, in which he expresses his belief about death. Though a Christian and a member of the United Reform Church, his poem has echoes of Buddhism in its doubts about the survival of individual, separate consciousness beyond death. The religious content could be seen in his faith that love is ultimate, so central to the Christian tradition. Buddhism, however, also elevates loving kindness as crucial to human development.

> When I die I shall cease to be
> That flawed clay vessel I once called me.
> My spirit like a drop of rain
> Will fall back into the sea again.
>
> Once held aloft by the living sun
> I fall in peace to the loving one.
> Once blasted by the winds above
> I merge into the sea of love.
>
> The dirt that made me falls away
> To make another me one day.
> The joy, the hope, the fear, the pain
> Will fill another jar again.
>
> But where I go there is no fear,
> And where I rest is very near.
> A sea of love where you can swim
> And let its healing warmth seep in.
>
> So do not search for me beyond
> I'm but one drop in that great pond.
> Not lost forevermore but free
> Not he nor you nor I but we.[6]

Increasingly the natural sciences are weaving a coherent and unified explanatory web for all phenomena, and some argue that the idea of an independent soul is more and more incredible and unimaginable. The mystery of death has always taken people to the edge of what can be imagined, and great efforts have been made to find the clues to whether death is the gateway to immortality or extinction. These include trying to make sense of the many descriptions of what have come to be known as 'near-death experiences.' Some of these include the 'great clarity of the patient's consciousness as he looks down on his body from outside, often observing exactly the frenzied efforts of the medical team to revive him.'[7] The accuracy of such reports were striking in that the level of knowledge of what went on would not be normally possessed by the patient, unless he had seen what actually occurred. Nevertheless, such records do not prove to the sceptic that life continues in some way after death. That remains in the field of faith and hope.

Death can be variously seen as helping to give meaning and perspective to our lives. It pushes us to re-evaluate what is really important and to give priority to that. Death is not simply the end of life, but the force that introduces a wholeness and unity into life, a wholeness which is often incomplete until we face our finitude. That seems to me the reason why some people who are dying have a peace and integrity about them which makes them humbling to be with. They have run their race. In the words of Teilhard de Chardin.

> The function of death is to provide the necessary entrance into our innermost selves.[8]

Some Personal Thoughts about the Meaning of Death

In the remainder of this chapter, a variety of people in our own time write of their sense of the meaning or meaninglessness of death. There is a diversity in contemporary culture, which is reflected in these observations. We can look, for example, in vain for any neat piety from the writer Tim Pears:

> Death makes no sense to me. I suppose its meaning can't be separated from the meaning of life. If life does have meaning then it must be part of a continuum, a journey of the soul, in which death, as both alarming prospect and ultimate eventuality, has an equally vital function.
>
> On the other hand, life (and death) may have no meaning whatsoever, beyond being part of a chaotic cosmic joke. In which case at

least there's a lot of good slapstick, some decent gags, and death makes for a fine punchline.

For those who are sceptical about survival after death, there is a sense that the person only lives on in memory and can be honoured by the impact they continue to have on those who survive: 'he whom we love and lose is no longer where he was before. He is now wherever we are.' In that way people are remembered through being mentioned casually or formally after their death, often in association with particular achievements to which they have contributed.

Mel Berger, a management consultant, struggling through the impact of the death of his wife Pam has written of his thoughts about Body and Spirit:

> What is death? Why does it happen to people we love, or to anyone? Is it foreordained and written down in an enormous book? Is it simply the result of cause-effect events, for example, by being hit by a car? Or is it a random event like being hit by lightning? There are at least two possible aspects of death, the death of the body and the death of the spirit. The death of the body is more understandable: we can see it, we can observe decay. We can dream of them, we can imagine them walking along the High Street, or even sitting in their favourite chair. We have seen skeletons, and so we can imagine what a dead body looks like. By comparison understanding the spirit is far more difficult to visualise.
>
> If the spirit dies along with the body, we are in a lonely position, especially in an urbanised culture. Life is over and that is that. The person can only live in the memories of others. It is, however, more hopeful to believe that the essence of the person remains, and that it is possible to retain contact in some way. I remember a visit from a beloved cousin in the form of a silhouette against a curtain after he had passed away, only I did not know that he had died at the time of the visit.
>
> If the spirit remains in some way alive, does the spiritual connection remain? If it does, it follows that it will remain with those you love and those you hate: 'I will haunt you for ever' is a threat that signals that the relationship is not over, although you may wish it were.
>
> What does the spirit do all day or however time is conceived on the other side? Perhaps it has its own work to do, past events and people to come to terms with and hopefully to keep a watchful eye towards those left behind and still in grief. Probably over time the need for the supportive contact decreases and people and spirits can get on with doing their own thing. Hopefully in times of need, it is possible to reconnect with your spiritual partner or friend.

Maybe it is possible to reincarnate together in the next life, an exciting and hopeful possibility. But how is the decision taken? And how is it decided where on earth, or not, that the next life is to be lived?

Maybe life and death are like being in a large television with lots of channels, so that we can tune into different people and spirits at different times. Or perhaps the spirit life is more free flowing: no agendas, diaries or appointments on the other side! But at the end I am left with a list of possibilities and questions, but no answers. I am totally baffled and short on faith, which I have heard used to justify too many contradictory beliefs. Instead of the faith that I want, which would feel too much like a highly biased bit of wish fulfilment, I have a void. If the pain of grief keeps going, maybe I will turn to religion or psychotherapy to achieve some healing.

After the catharsis of bereavement, what is left is loneliness, the sense of being alone in the universe. Is that the human condition? Maybe I have reached the point that I need to take more initiatives to refind my connections with people or at least to prop up some hopefully temporary inner subsidence!

Bill Merrington, a Warwickshire vicar, shows how the struggle to make sense of death and dying is not avoided by having a Christian faith:

I think that sometimes that we confuse the issue between after-life and heaven with death. Although death may well be the gateway through which we pass into the other life, it is also a destructive gateway. It is (a) a process of decay, although not spiritually, certainly physically and mentally. How can this be good? (b) It is a severing of relationships, of one's history and sense of belonging on this earth. This too can be painful and damaging. When I therefore see a 97-year-old lady in a nursing home, who may well be looking forward to dying in the sense of entering a peace and an after-life, I am observing the process of death itself, which comes through the accumulation of disease and of the destruction of the body. So when people say 'Oh it is release from their illness and pains and weariness', what they are actually saying is that it is a release from their process of death.

We often use the word death in two different ways. At one point we are talking about it being the end, being destructive and of being separated, while at the same time using the word death as a means of escape from these very things into a new life. For those left behind, death in most cases can only be seen in a negative light which is why we end up with the whole issue of grief. Death brings the severing of affectionate bonds or attachment in the case of children, which inevitably causes a reaction within those who remain. It also brings the recognition that the process of death is in fact taking place within us all. Medicine and science attempt to remove death from our community, but if it is such a good thing, why is it then that we spend millions on attempting to remove it?

Anna, a primary school teacher and mother, writes from the perspective of one who lost her mother as a young child and then as a young adult both her grandparents, who had helped fill that maternal vacuum as she grew up:

The main thing death means to me is separation. The things that are most important, and what give me most happiness, are relationships. Death has brought about the end of my relationships with three pivotal people in my life. Because of my religious beliefs, I hope that death is not the end of everything, but it has certainly caused very painful separations.

I hope that death means the gateway onto another plane of existence, but I find the thought of being separated from all who mean most to me unbearable. It feels that it will make any kind of existence meaningless. Life must also be about developing my inner self, or finding out more about it and also my relationship with God, so that I will be better able to cope with separation when the time comes.

My first experience of death was when my mother died. I was too young to understand it or remember, but it has influenced my whole life ever since. I grew up with her absence a daily feature of my life, despite the love I had from my father and grandparents. I looked for her wherever I went, hoping to see her ghost and dreamed of her return frequently. She was spoken about a lot and so I had a clear picture of her, but she was also very mysterious. I felt that I would never match up to her, as death sanctifies people, especially when they die young. So she was to me, as a child, flawless in beauty and intellect and larger than life in strength of personality. She seemed more real and solid than I ever did, until recently. More than 30 years later, I am still experiencing new feelings about her death.

When Kay Walker, a hospice counsellor, reflects on the impact on her of her father's death, Death itself warrants a capital letter, as if it is a person or a kind of God with whom she is struggling to come to terms. She also expresses that tension that other people sometimes feel between seeing Death as a friend or as an enemy, or even paradoxically both at the same time:

Death means two things for me – it means people I love leaving me and it means me leaving people I love. The deaths of other people, apart from the people I love and me, is a distant thing but it touches me in the way that John Donne's bell did. It reminds me of losing the people I love – or of them having to lose me.

My work is with people and endings. It has been for some years, both with people who are dying and with those left behind when their loved ones die. I've known in my head and my mind and even a bit in my heart what death is about – but now I've lost one of the most important people in my life, I am coming to know Death with every cell in my body. I am not enjoying it but it is one of the most powerful experiences I have known. It is like having a child in that way ... powerful, empowering and wonderful. Its empowering because nothing else matters when you're in the midst of it. It's more painful than childbirth because the pain goes on and on. I know instinctively that I will carry the pain of my father's death in my heart until I die myself.

I don't know if I shall join him when I die. I feel as he did, that I cannot remember anything before I was born and will probably not know anything after I die. So I feel it's best to say all we have to say, do all we have to do and love all we have to love, while we're still alive.

I'm learning that the magical strength I thought I had from him is now in me. A part of me died when he did, but a part of him carries on in me now. I feel good when I recognise some small good thing I do that is like some things he used to do – or even some small not-so-good thing – and I feel proud to be alive, to be like him, and to be me.

My father was cremated after he died. I sprinkled some of his ashes in a river and on the land in an important place for me. I look forward to going back there to visit that river and that land. I hope my children will sprinkle some of my ashes there too.

I'm glad I have lived and am alive. I know I will miss my children and other people I love when it is time to die but I am not afraid of Death. I don't look forward to it – but I think it will be good, like Birth and like Life.

Richard Worsley, a counselling trainer, reflects that:

When I am most aware of the immediate, I fear death the least. I have God. I believe in Resurrection. I may be wholly wrong and I face that. If I am wrong, I will meet that (or not!), with equanimity. Yet, I want never to deny the power of the existential angst of death.

Angst, a German word, means the sadness or anxiety that comes with reflecting on the human condition. There is often plenty of angst in contemplating death.

Judyann Roblee, a musician based in Germany, thinks of her struggle with belief and doubt as her ideas change over the years:

I have found that my ideas and thoughts about death have altered and changed shape enormously during my life. I expect that will continue as I get even older. I remember my first thoughts of death as a very small child. At that time it was more of a physical picture in the imagination. Of course, I didn't *think* about it much, and it certainly had nothing to do with me. But the word 'death' conjured up corkscrewing worms turning in the earth. Why worms? I rather enjoyed worms and freshly turned earth. I can still get in touch with this feeling particularly during an aria in Handel's *Messiah*, where the singer sings 'And worms shall eat your body', with a wonderful 'worming' accompaniment in the orchestra!

I think what I did was more an effort to defend myself from the unknown. If birth was a natural phenomena about which we remembered nothing, death must also be a natural act and somehow we would be prepared and ready for it – as though it would be instinctual. I *still* hope that there might be a feeling of completeness and a readiness to move on at the time of death. But I was disabused of this idea on asking a friend of mine with strong faith who was dying of cancer if he felt these things.

As I get older life becomes *more* precious each season. At 25 I would have died gratefully, I couldn't bear the thought of being 50 or so. But now I am in my sixties, as I look at the reality of, hopefully, 10 or 20 more seasons, I wish for much longer!

What about the 'life of the world to come'? A phrase we have used all our lives if our lives are lived within the church. This is a hard one to grasp as a real belief for me. What is it? What does it mean? And will I like it? I have had one or two dreams of such strength that I have woken up thinking 'this is what it must be like!'. A pouring out of happiness and grief, a release from everything, a joyful peacefulness. I value these dreams tremendously, as being a possible glimpse of the world to come. I wonder too, if there is nothing, a sort of 'lights out' feeling. I fight against this because it seems that I lack faith and perhaps this last leap into the unknown is the greatest leap of faith that we have to take.

From Annie and Titus Mercer, parents and teachers who practice Transcendental Meditation:

Relief, liberation, adventure, expansion, revelation, new birth, fear of sickness / infirmity / loneliness / leaving loved ones, freedom, reunion with loved ones, into light / infinity / unity / divinity .... These words conjure up some of the kaleidoscope of emotions and thoughts associated with death for us.

Coexistence of opposites, that's life (and death).

When individuals try to work out what death means for them, some go on their own journey of exploration into the unknown, often drawing on the ideas, metaphors and myths of their own culture. They may go into poetic orbit with a mystical and exciting belief in the paradox of hope:

Only when you drink from the river of silence
  shall you indeed sing.
And when you have reached the mountain top,
  then you shall begin to climb.
And when the earth shall claim your limbs,
  then shall you truly dance.[10]

But they may also forge ahead with new ideas that may echo
other traditions as they go deep into the well of human experience, thought and imagination. Others stick firmly to what they
know or believe to be known. For them, any hope of some kind of
personal survival beyond death is essentially a human creation,
for which there is no evidence. It is a natural expression of the
powerful desire and drive to exist, to live and not to come to a full
stop.

Notes

1. Bayley, John *Iris: A Memoir of Iris Murdoch* (Duckworth, London 1998).

2. De Hennezel, M. *Intimate Death: how the dying teach us to live* (Little, Brown and Company, London 1997).

3. Simon, Paul *George on My Mind*, a tribute to Gershwin on his centenary (*The Observer Review*, London 6 September 1998).

4. Poll, M *Religion in Britain* (Now, London, 21 December 1979).

5. From a tombstone quoted by Spence, Christopher *A Homecoming and the Harvest* (Lifestory, London 1979).

6. Burne, Simon *When I die I Shall Cease to Be* (unpublished, Rugby, 1999).

7. Badham, Paul and Linda *Immortality or Extinction?* (Macmillan, London, 1982).

8. The Bishop of St.German's, *Speech to the Help the Hospices Conference* (17 November 1998).

9. de Chardin, Pierre Teilhard, *Le Milieu Divin*, (Collins, London 1960).

12

Preparing for Dying and Death

- Facing Death Together or Alone
- The Tasks of Preparing for Death
- The Emotional Response to Dying
- Supporting the Dying
- The Healing Process
- Active and Passive Responses to Dying

It is sometimes said that sudden death is the 'best way to go', but it can also be very hard on close family and friends because it gives them no time to prepare. Consider the alternative of a protracted death from the dying person's point of view, however. While it may provide others with the opportunity to prepare themselves for their loss, the dying person encounters what for some can be the hardest of tasks: facing one's own death. Knowing that you are dying, especially if you have not yet come to terms with it, is hard enough. It can be made even harder if those around maintain a conspiracy of silence, so that the dying person feels shut out and even more isolated.

For some, on the other hand, prolonged denial is their preferred way of coping and they do not want to be faced with the truth of their condition. Doctors, nurses and relatives have to tread a fine line, picking out the signals of what the dying person really wants to know and talk about. In the past collusion with denial was the norm, but today more people are saying that to know the truth is what they want in order to base their plans and their strategy of their skirmish with death in reality rather than fantasy.

Some hope that death will occur after a period in which they can manage the end of their life awarely, tying up the loose ends and saying their farewells properly. Some Native American people have a belief that the way a person dies tells the story of how he lived. Dying is a living art, the beginning of a further passage to something new and unknown.[1]

Facing Death Together or Alone

The experience of many who work with the dying is that the latter often know that they are dying even when those closest to them assume the opposite. This assumption may be based on the fact that they have not talked together openly on honestly about death for fear of upsetting each other.

> When the dying person knows that he is dying, what is needed is some help to articulate that knowledge. Why should it be so hard to say? Isn't it because everyone else's distress makes it hard to talk, and so the dying person has to protect them? ... Our experience confirms that the person who says 'I am going to die' does not become the victim of death, but rather the protagonist in his or her own dying. It is a moment of standing up straight again, and of the return of an inner strength that nobody else knew was there. (Charles-Edwards, 1983)

But even if that is the way they usually communicate, there is a case for changing the pattern now, because facing death alone can be extremely daunting. To share thoughts and feelings on this issue can bring to the surface the love and commitment, often unspoken, which underpins the relationship. Not to share something as important as the imminent death of a partner can be a tragic epilogue to a relationship; all the more so where the norm is mutual openness.

There are, however, many people who are alone on the road to death. Some patients in hospital have no visitors. Funerals take place with no one in attendance. It is all too easy for people to become isolated in a highly mobile, urban society in which people struggle to discover a sense of community. In many partnerships one person is left who may die alone, especially if an extended family does not exist nearby. Although we cannot share the actual experience of dying, being with someone when they die can feel profoundly supportive.

> The person who sees death coming has no time to lose. He or she will engage with full force and needs to feel this being reciprocated. I try to make my doubting colleague understand how indispensable the presence of another human being is. There has

to be someone else to share this ultimate experience of connection – someone emotionally open, who will not shy away; someone who can remain open to these emotional demands without feeling threatened. This is precisely what those around the dying often find hard to bear, and if they run away so often, it's because they don't understand the meaning of this sudden vitality and they're afraid it can drag them into death as well.[1]

The Tasks of Preparing for Death

Practical Tasks

Death comes to us all, some expectedly and some suddenly and out of the blue; so part of growing up and growing older is to face up to our own mortality realistically. Undertaking the practical tasks is also a means of preparing emotionally, because those tasks involve growing out of denial: 'why bother, it may never happen', even though we know that it will. Of all these tasks, failing to make a will can be the greatest nuisance and (where there are young children) failure to those left behind; but all the items in the box warrant attention, if you care at all for those close to you.

Deal with them, the sooner the better: any one of us could be struck down today.

Are you adequately insured?

If you are paying a mortgage, would the outstanding payments be covered in the event of your death? Would your partner have enough to live on if your (separate) accounts were frozen on your death? Does he or she know where this information is to be found?

Have you made a will?

Forms are available from some stationers or newsagents, if you want to prepare a simple one and to avoid the expense of going though a solicitor. They must be completed correctly and signed in the presence of witnesses. Do your close relatives or friends, at least your executors, know where to find the will?

Children under the age of 18

Do your close family or friends know where the will is to be found? If you have children under the age of 18 and have not specified who you wish to be their legal guardians, the local Department of Social Services will need to decide who should look after them. If it is not obvious to them who are suitable guardians, the children may be put into care.

Have you discussed funeral arrangements?

Sometimes these questions seem too painful to consider and they are just left to the next-of-kin when the time comes.

In the event of your death, your next-of-kin will need to make these arrangements quickly. Would they know whether you wish to be cremated or buried and what kind of funeral you would want. If you are to be cremated, would you want your ashes to be buried in the crematorium or in another special place. Even if there may be difficulty in burying ashes in various places, there is likely to be little objection to them being scattered discreetly in a beautiful place you love, perhaps in the countryside or at sea. Is there to be a plaque or sign in your memory somewhere, so that those who grieve have somewhere to visit, if they wish?

They may be helped if they have been told by you of some favourite music or hymns or readings that you would like to be included in the funeral. Even better, if it is written down, so that they do not have to rely on remembering a conversation from the dim, distant past on the subject. You could take the trouble to write some brief notes down on the subject yourself.

Where are your important documents?

Do those close to you know where they are, and are they safe?

What about the practical side of home life? If only one of a partnership is competent, it may be time for the other one to learn where the stop cock and the fuse box are, and to take a turn in defrosting the refrigerator or doing a load of washing.

Are there things you need/want to say, practical or emotional, and to whom?

It can be extremely important to some people that the person who has died told them how much they liked or loved them, or what they valued or appreciated about them, and also made it possible in reverse. It may also be very important for the bereaved to know that they have said the same kind of thing to the deceased.

The Psychological Task

Underpinning the practical questions, there are the psychological tasks of preparing for death. At one level, this is a lifetime's work, albeit often at an unconscious level; but if we become aware that our death is getting nearer, it becomes a higher and more urgent priority and nearer the surface of our consciousness. The tasks of preparing for death have been summarised by Sylvia Poss (1981) in six parts:

1. To become aware of impending death;
2. To balance hope and fear throughout the crises;
3. To take an active decision to reverse the physical survival processes in order to die;
4. To relinquish responsibility and physical independence;
5. To separate the self from former experiences;
6. To prepare emotionally and spiritually for death.

Not every dying person will need to complete all of these, nor will the process necessarily operate at a conscious level. The tasks involve letting go of this life and, especially in the final two, disengaging from it. At a certain stage, not easy to pinpoint, the dying person may need to stop fighting to get well or even survive. Attachment to life here and now will consequently weaken and lose interest for this person. If it is not understood as part of a natural process, this withdrawal from life can feel like rejection and can hurt those being left behind.

Amy had been coping superbly with Jack's long illness, caring for him and keeping the job and home going, until recently when she seemed very moody and depressed. In the office one lunch hour, a colleague asked her how Jack was, commenting that Amy had seemed low lately. Amy described how her husband had always taken such a close interest in the family but latterly seemed to be ceasing to do so. It was as if he was beginning to withdraw from life before he died. To Amy it felt as if he did not love the family or her so much after all. Perhaps he had never loved her through all those years when she had believed that their marriage was so good. But none of this was true. Jack's behaviour was not an expression of how he felt towards the family. His attention was being drawn irrevocably to his departure from this world. In this way the separation which death was to bring was already making its presence felt.

A great deal of emotional and spiritual energy is required for the work of preparing for death. It is like getting ready for emigration or a world cruise, only more so! The preparation can get in the way of the farewells.

Balancing Hope and Fear

The focus of hope and fear switches successively from the possibility of recovery, to the quality of life remaining before death, on to the manner of dying and what happens afterwards. Attention may slide backwards and forwards from one to the other and it is not surprising if perspectives begin to change. When in ordinary life we are hurt or ill, our attention is naturally drawn from where it was to the pain in order to maximise the chances of healing occurring. How much more will this apply when we encounter life's most momentous event?

The Emotional Response to Dying

The six tasks mentioned above are often accompanied by a process of mood changes. Though not the same as in bereavement (see chapter 6), these tasks bear some similarity to that process. In both cases the switch from one state to another may be difficult to predict. But this does not mean that the dying person is going round in emotional circles. The process involves different feelings being dominant at different times. It is as if it is too much to experience them all simultaneously. 'Human kind cannot bear very much reality' (Eliot, 1940), at least not all at once.

The emotional stages those who are dying often go through, although not necessarily in this order, can be summarised as (Kubler-Ross, 1973 and Charles-Edwards, 1983):

- shock
- denial and isolation
- anger
- bargaining
- depression and sadness
- fear
- regression
- acceptance or resignation

No one even hinted to Alan that he was dying even though he was so ill that, as a former soccer player on the right side of 40, he could not even wash himself. He seemed to discourage his family from talking realistically and actively planned a trip to Australia to see his brother's family. For his sake, his family here went along with the idea, even though they thought it was totally unrealistic. They assured the hospice staff that he had no notion that he might be terminally ill, and that in their view it was best for him that way. Shortly after his admission, while being bathed by a nurse, Alan started to talk about his condition with insight and knowledge. He cried a lot about the loss of his life and what this would mean for his family. But as he got out of the bath he indicated that he did not want to upset them unduly and started to talk again about the trip to Adelaide.

Denial is a coping mechanism which protects not only the dying person but also other people, sometimes as much or even more. To talk realistically to everyone may be too painful. As time passes, some people want to talk more honestly but find they cannot. Talking can, for some, detoxify their fear. Because of this, a person who appears to be in an extended phase of total denial may respond with great relief and openness to being asked 'How do you feel about your illness now?' Such a question can feel like being granted permission to talk openly.

Someone who is terminally ill may want to protect those close to them from being too upset. They may fear being avoided or shunned, if being with them is too depressing. On the other hand, denial is not just avoiding reality: it can also affirm reality. Being ill and close to death is not the only reality. The reason for not wanting to hasten death is the pleasure and interest they may be experiencing about being alive in this world, with all its faults and all the problems of the illness.

There was a gloomy character in the British radio comedy ITMA years ago, whose catch phrase was 'It's being so cheerful that keeps me going'. The joke was that this was the opposite of what she was really like. Some well-meaning friends, eager not to collude with denial, can be most depressing by homing in on the illness or accident, its treatment (or lack of treatment) and all that is most painful about the situation. They may think that they are sympathising, but are spreading a sense of despair and victim-hood. Whereas the person they are visiting may want desperately to get their attention out and onto all kinds of other subjects.

On the other hand, there is the opposite trap of refusing to acknowledge the person's condition and missing or ignoring the verbal or non-verbal signals indicating that the person wanted to talk about their situation and even to be supported in their coming to terms with their mortality. What the dying person needs and deserves from those trying to support them is, if nothing else, the willingness to listen properly, to hear and notice what is being communicated, non-verbally as well as through words, and to pick up and maybe check out the cues.

Denial provides some temporary protection against the natural emotional pain in most of these stages. It hurts to feel angry or sad or frightened. Most people need to use denial to some degree, especially when the imminence of death has been first acknowledged.

But denial can outlive its usefulness. When it forms a barrier to communication between people who have otherwise had an open and close relationship, it needs to be gently challenged. For others it becomes a firmly held strategy to the end and is best respected.

> I shaved my father with his own razor, slipping glances at his eyes. His pale grey eyes were even paler, farther away. They made me think of Gorky's description of the dying Tolstoy: 'He listens attentively as though recalling something which he has forgotten, or as for something new and unknown'.[2]

Supporting the Dying

Colleagues and friends will be able to give better support when they know the nature of the main tasks facing the dying person and/or partner. Lacking this knowledge they may find themselves minimising or weakening the available support. For example, they may:

1) pretend that nothing out of the ordinary is happening;
2) belittle their hope or fear and reinforce the sense that you can feel hope *or* fear, but not both at the same time;
3) tell them to keep on fighting when it is no longer appropriate;
4) imply that their respect is tied to the dying person's determination, courage and success in looking after himself or herself;
5) imply that to let go and even to die might be a kind of failure;
6) hint that it was still their responsibility to think about and even take responsibility for their 'dependants' at home or at work;
7) disapprove or show embarrassment when the person reflects on death.

Listening can be distorted through all kinds of ideological filters. Sometimes there may be a variation of a religious 'Catch

22'. If your faith is strong enough, you will recover and if you do not, the life after death is better than this one. So you have no excuse for being gloomy. If you are, then you have a problem with your faith: it is just not good enough.

> Alice knew how seriously ill she was. She had given up work and had a bed made up in the living room because she could no longer manage the stairs. Friends from the church met with her to pray for her recovery, sure that it was God's will that she should get better if only they could all have enough faith. Her husband was not so 'religious' but he welcomed their support at such a critical time. He encouraged Alice to 'fight' and not give up hope. That seemed essential if she was to have any chance of recovery. Alice did her best, but could sense that her condition was deteriorating; this made her feel more and more inadequate and guilty. Eventually she rebelled and pleaded with them to give her some support so that she could do three things: prepare for death, think about the future of her children after it and begin the heart-breaking task of letting them go. The response of her friends and husband was at first negative. Unaware, they were wrapping in a cloak of piety their inability to face Alice's death. Slowly, Alice helped them gain insight into this so that they could begin to support her in the way that she needed.

The great grief of leaving behind highly dependent young children may be reinforced by guilt. Sharing some of the pain of that guilt and helping the dying one to think through the best arrangements possible after death may be important ways of supporting someone. On the other hand, if it is too painful to think in detail about the children's future, it may be more important to decide who is to have responsibility subsequently, and then to concentrate on communicating with them and trusting them to do their best.

This can be a crucial part, at the right time, of 'letting go'. Nevertheless, it may be too painful to make a rational decision as to who is to care for the children after a mother dies, and the matter has to be decided by others following her death. This is in part because the decision may depend on some sensitive and detailed consultation with various people, a task which may be beyond her physically and emotionally.

Different questions present themselves in different circumstances. If the parent that is dying is the main breadwinner, the future financial support of the family may be a crucial element in looking at the potential family and friendship resources needed by the children as they grow up, beyond what insurance cover may provide.

The Healing Process

If we are angry, our teeth and fists clench and we want to shout, roar or strike out. If we are frightened, our body may shake, we may sweat and so on. If we are sad, we may weep. In some societies children and adults are encouraged to express feelings without inhibition. It is assumed that it is natural – 'Better out than in' and 'Better to get if off your chest'.

Unfortunately our culture has been contaminated by the opposing idea exemplified in the British 'stiff upper lip'. The well-meaning intention behind this is that if someone is demonstrating the physical signs of pain, such as shedding tears, crying out, raging or laughter, which may verge at times on the hysterical, the kindest thing is to stop him or her. There are two rationalisations at work behind this idea:

'If you can stop the symptoms, you help to stop the pain'. But the opposite is nearer the truth: if you stop the expression of pain, it can become locked in and more difficult to release. Holding back the feelings can in itself cause added stress, whereas to express them can bring a sense of release, which can dissipate tension and help the person relax a little, notwithstanding their situation.

'It is somehow weak or in the case of men, unmanly, to express strong feelings: weak people are feminine feelings-dominated and illogical thinkers. The strong masculine person, of either gender, has feelings well in place and can, therefore, think clearly and logically'. This split way of regarding human functioning sees emotion and thought as virtually in opposition to each other, rather than regarding our feelings as part of our intelligence, providing us with valuable information and energy. Recent emphasis on 'emotional intelligence' aimed at a wider, more balanced approach has sparked its own backlash, in which the fear is expressed that society is in danger of sinking into a sentimental abyss of sloppy thinking with a new respect for emotion.

A New Model of Strength

We need a new model of strength to replace the image of the brittle, highly-controlled man who locks away his feelings through repression and alcohol. A deeper strength is discovered by acknowledging vulnerability rather than hiding it. The release of tension can clear rather than cloud the mind.

The idea that expressing pain somehow makes it worse may have a grain of truth in it. It can be superficially harder for people near them – family, colleagues, friends, clergy, nurses and doctors – who may prefer to pretend that it is much less upsetting than it really is. It can be most uncomfortable to be close to someone who is raging or grieving without inhibition. But what this highlights is the need for support for all of the key people near a dying person, rather than a conspiratorial atmosphere of silence and pretence.

There are times when we need to control our feelings, perhaps even to disguise how we feel, but there are also times when we need to be ourselves, 'a time to weep and a time to laugh', a time for emotional openness and honesty as well as a time for reticence and restraint.

Our emotions are part of us: they are no more obsolete than our kidneys or elbows. Whole people with their full potential have and need the capacity to be happy, sad, frightened and angry. If they are, then they will naturally laugh, cry, rage, tremble, sweat and yawn.

People who are dying do not need a culture of repression around them at that point in their lives. Happily, there are many parents, teachers and others with responsibility for young people who do not inflict on them such lies as 'big boys don't cry!' or 'showing strong emotion is unbecoming to a woman'.

Active and Passive Responses to Dying

Our feelings are what give us the motivation we need to act decisively and with dignity in the face of our own death. Sometimes we need to be highly active in fighting a disease or reaching out in love to someone important to us. Sometimes, however, we may need to be more passive, if the time comes to let go of the struggle to live.

In the range of tasks the dying face, passivity may at times be as crucial and worthy of our support as being proactive. A paradox of dying is that the last and hardest demonstration of our maturity may be how well we collaborate in letting go of the independence that we have slowly achieved since our birth. Those who come to accept that they are now as physically dependent on others as they were when they were a baby may be showing a strength no less great for its passivity. It deserves our admiration as much as any more active heroic feat.

Even more than our encouragement to fight against death, the dying colleague may at some stage need our support in the hard business of letting go of life.

Notes

1. De Hennezel, M. *Intimate Death*: *How the Dying Teach Us to Live*, (Little, Brown, London 1997).

2. Dodson, James *Final Rounds*: *Father, Son, the Golf Journey of a Lifetime* (Arrow Books, London 1997).

13
Ignoring Death

- The Death of Death?
- Death Happens to other People!
- The Death Taboo
- Unhelpful Attitudes towards Death

The Death of Death?

Dying is helped by many constructive influences within our culture, but the fear of death also tempts people to create a fantasy in which it does not exist: an ideological structure for collective, cultic denial! There are some that even argue that dying is unnecessary and avoidable, if only we achieve the correct combination of physical and spiritual health. It is not helped by the Christian belief that Christ has conquered death, as if the kind of death being discussed is the same as the mortality which is the focus of this book. The death of death would be an unmitigated disaster for the human race, as it would presumably not be accompanied by the death of birth. Any theoretical commitment to bio-diversity, to sharing our planet with other species, has been drastically sabotaged by the escalating human population explosion of the 20th century, which leaves less and less room for people, let alone other animals, as we squeeze greater numbers into smaller spaces.

Death Happens to other People!

Our 20th century western society reinforces the sense that death is something that happens to other people, if at all, in several ways. Our Victorian forebears in Britain were closer to death as part of ordinary life, as are many people living in other countries in the contemporary world. Advances in environmental health and medicine mean that it will be longer before death makes its claim on most of us. The time is fast approaching when one in five living in the UK will be a pensioner and a tenth of our population over 75 years old. So many people can live on in old age without the preoccupation with death that was difficult to avoid in the past. Finally, our sensitivity to death can, paradoxically, be dulled by repeated exposure through the media to images of war, violent death, dismembered bodies, and so on.

The Death Taboo

The taboo on death involves ignoring or avoiding the subject or talking about it as indirectly as possible. Some of the rituals of death in Britain tend to deny the reality of death. Bodies are removed from hospital wards in trolleys with false bottoms so that people do not realise that a corpse is being carried past them. If a hearse and funeral cortège pass down the street it is no longer customary for pedestrians to stop in respect and solidarity with the mourners. It is often disregarded, with other motorists passing as if it was any other vehicle.

Euphemisms are still commonly used in talking about death: 'he passed on,' 'fell asleep' or less respectfully, 'is pushing up the daisies'. The tendency to replace blunt or direct expressions with mild or vague ones can be a form of denial. If you are with someone who is dying or has been bereaved, there is often a dilemma – how to avoid talking about the topic most on both your minds. It can be resolved ahead of time by keeping clear of the person or by making a rapid exit. The dying and bereaved may notice that they are being avoided by some people and that others are embarrassed in their presence and are clearly relieved to get away from them. By naming death unambiguously it is less easy to avoid its reality.

Unhelpful Attitudes towards Death

These include:

- death is an evil to be defeated by science or religion, whereas birth is good;
- 'suffering is minimised by avoiding the subject of death'. This attitude is not well founded. Suffering may actually be increased, because the person concerned feels more isolated;
- 'the physical reality of death is more distressing than the imag-

ined reality'; On the contrary, except where there has been serious facial injury, being with the dead body can be helpful in coming to terms with the reality of death and beginning the healing process of mourning.

14

Choosing when to Die:
Suicide and Euthanasia

- Helping to Prevent Avoidable Suicide
- The Impact of Suicide on Bereavement
- An Overview of Suicide
- Stress and Work
- Bullying at Work
- Young People At Risk
- Suicide, Work, Unemployment and Men
- Suicide and Money
- Voluntary Euthanasia or Assisted Suicide

Helping to Prevent Avoidable Suicide

This chapter considers suicide and some of the ways in which work impacts on it and vice versa. Work stress can trigger or contribute to a suicide attempt, some of which are successful. A good manager ensures as far as possible that the right equipment and machinery are in the right place at the right time and well serviced and maintained to do the job. How much more do people need to be cared for rather than wasted as a valuable investment? It is no less the responsibility of the organisation and line manager to ensure that are in good working order and not liable to break down. Unlike machinery, people have a life, with its hopes, despair and stresses, away from the job, over which the employer has minimum influence. Nevertheless, the responsible manager will:

- be alert to such stresses which may overload the individual, if pressures are also building up at work at the same time;
- not ignore staff mentioning that they are feeling that they can no longer cope or feel trapped in an impossible situation;
- never ignore people who express thoughts about suicide, allowing them to talk about it never caused a suicide but might have prevented a few;

- beware of and avoid piling up pressure towards breaking point on individuals;
- take account of the different levels of resilience and coping mechanisms among staff;
- respect and take account of their responsibilities to others outside work, especially to children, other dependent relatives and neighbours;
- build a culture in which people are encouraged and affirmed as well as challenged;
- promote a management style in which bullying and harassment are out of order;
- be open to the possibility of careful and informed referral to counselling or other appropriate help, internal or external.

The Impact of Suicide on Bereavement

On one level suicide is just another bereavement for those close to the person and all that applies to bereavement in general is likely to apply to them, but of course it is not the same. When a person who was seriously, perhaps terminally, ill, takes there own life, it may be experienced, as usually is the intention, as hastening what might otherwise be a miserable death rather than as suicide. In cases where death is thought to be by suicide, some or all of the following points tend to apply:

- An overwhelming sense of horror and shock at what the person has done and often the manner in which it was done, for example, finding someone close to you hanging;
- Guilt and a sense of responsibility for supposedly failing the person in some way, for example, in not anticipating or sensing what was in their mind, in minimising their distress and somehow not making things better for them;
- Guilt, in some cases, at an element of relief that a person, who may have been abusive or depressing to be with, has taken their own life;
- Anger that the person has done this, perhaps leaving the bereaved person to cope on their own with the trauma, that they have opted out of by escaping through the gateway of death;
- Unresolved problems, for example, financial, perhaps caused by gambling, heavy drinking or the use of other drugs, caring for disabled or other dependent relatives or problems with parenting, can be made worse by the suicide of one partner, leaving the other on their own to struggle on.
- Shame that they did not prevent or even worse that they may have, in some way albeit indirectly, caused the suicide. This can be particularly acute for some of those with strong religious convictions;

– Many describe the feeling of being tainted by the stigma of suicide. They feel that others are making all kinds of assumptions about their relationship, condemning them and being very wary of them.

Many of those bereaved through a suicide feel isolated, especially as most people have never been close to anyone else in that situation. For that reason reading about the experience of other people bereaved by suicide, such as Alison Wertheimer's book, *A Special Scar*,[1] can be helpful.

An Overview of Suicide

Today suicide accounts for about a third of the external causes of death in the UK, about 70% more than for road traffic accidents. In 1996, it was estimated that 5,905 people committed suicide, an average of one every 90 minutes, and about a further 100,000 attempt to kill themselves every year. Nevertheless, the level of suicides is not out of kilter with other countries, despite the French writer Montaigne attributing suicide as the English disease because (according to Madame de Stael) the English were so impetuous and influenced by the opinion of others! The statistics are likely to be an underestimate because the cause of death of a number of people who kill themselves is recorded as something else, either to protect the surviving mourners or because the doctor may not be sure. Arguably in the case of terminal illness, the latter is the real cause of death even if the actual death has been by suicide. Some of those who are seriously depressed feel that life itself is a terminal condition, which of course it is.

People occasionally make the choice to die. There are many reasons for taking such a drastic step. Extreme anxiety, shame, depression or physical illness are some of the common triggers: feeling that the future is bleak and without hope. Nevertheless, none of these in themselves explain suicide, because there are others in similar desperate straits who soldier on, sometimes apparently against all the odds. The will to live is deep and powerful, but on the other hand, we also have to come to terms with the fact that one way or another we are going to die. Our death is as inevitable and natural as our birth, and so some people begin to think of death as an option in the face of calamity. To seek help to die, voluntary euthanasia, raises further issues, not least because it is illegal in most countries, including the UK.

There is a separate section on this issue at the end of the chapter.

Occasionally someone will kill themselves, rather than other people, for a cause: suicide becomes a sacrifice. Others may put themselves in extreme danger, so that they know that they are risking their life. Posthumous Victoria Crosses are sometimes awarded to such men. Unarmed protesters who stand in front of Chinese or Soviet tanks or self-immolating Buddhist monks protesting against the occupation of Tibet are also modern examples of the heroism that 'gives its life' for others. Jesus of Nazareth, Gandhi and Martin Luther King are famous examples of being prepared to offer the supreme sacrifice, knowing that they were putting their lives in danger by doing what they believed was right. The west porch of Westminster Abbey in London now has twelve statues in what were empty niches to 20th century martyrs from around the world.

Nevertheless, the taking of your own life in Britain has been widely condemned in the past. Until 1961, it was illegal and failed suicides were liable to be charged as soon as they recovered. There was a widespread belief that suicide was a sin, as well as a crime: the Roman Catholic Church taught that it was a mortal sin, meaning that the person was destined to go more or less straight to hell. The Church of England used to forbid the burial of someone who had committed suicide in hallowed ground. Instead the body was liable to be buried at a crossroads, with a stake driven 'through the heart' for good measure. The last such burial was recorded in 1823 in London's Hobart Place near Buckingham Palace.[2] Fortunately, in the past 150 years society and the Churches have both moved on from such an unforgiving and judgmental attitude. Although the Vatican's 1980 Declaration on Euthanasia observed that suffering has a special place in God's saving plan, few priests today would withhold their pastoral care to someone who took the matter into their own hands.

The personnel director telephoned the workplace counsellor: 'Do you remember our branch manager, Ian, you saw a couple of years ago? Well, I am afraid he resigned shortly after that, and has had a pretty rough couple of years by all accounts. I have just heard that he committed suicide last week, and I want to offer some sessions with you to his widow, if she wants them. Is that OK with you?' His widow had also worked for the company, but not for the past 8 years, while she concentrated on bringing up her three children. The counsellor remembered that he had tried to help with the increasing mess Ian was in, both at home and at work. Before booze had befuddled him, he had been a high flying executive and the company's attitude was forgiving. They wanted him to sort himself out for their sake as well as his, quite apart from the fact that he had married a delightful and popular member of staff, who was having a very rough time. But it had not worked out. Nevertheless, after the tragedy of Ian's death, the company had been imaginative and concerned enough to offer support to an ex-employee. Their gesture as much as the counselling, which she accepted, meant a lot to her at a particularly low point in her life.

Nevertheless, suicide is still regarded by some, if not as a crime or a mortal sin, then as a sign of mental unbalance. In a standard textbook for medical students, published in 1991, the observation was written that 'Suicide is no longer an offence, but properly considered as a manifestation of mental abnormality'. Coroners, recording a suicide verdict, often add while the balance of his or her mind was disturbed. The assumption is still widespread that it is inconceivable that someone thinking rationally could decide to end their own life. Life is so precious that most of us cling on to it at almost all costs. In contrast the uncertainty of what lies beyond death means that many of us hanker, without a great deal of hope, like Woody Allen, for a return ticket.

In a study published by the Samaritans,[3] a quarter of the population is estimated to have experienced someone close to them dying through suicide. Of these 11% said the person was a work colleague and 29% a friend, some of whom may have also been a friend at work. In general suicide rates have been slowly declining in the UK, although in recent years there has been an upsurge in suicide by young men in the 15-24 age bracket, which is 25% higher than the overall figures for men in general.

Stress and Work

The Cost of Stress, and Suicide Risk

The changing nature of work has lead many people to experience work overload, long working hours, job insecurity and a range of other stress causing problems in the workplace. This has meant that, over the past few years, many more employees are experiencing higher levels of depression, anxiety and a range of symptoms with which they are unable to cope.

Organisations depend on the existence of healthy staff who are capable of performing their work efficiently. The more successful companies in Britain today pay attention to the health and safety needs of their personnel, recognising that if their structures, policies and working practices reflect the needs of their employees it will increase both quality and output. The Samaritans is the bedrock for all those suffering from stress and depression who need social support and nurture.

Professor Cary Cooper of UMIST[4]

There are some particularly high risk occupations. The reasons for this include some combination of high stress, isolation and access to resources with which it is easier to kill ourselves. The importance of the last has been highlighted by the apparent link between the number of suicides among men in particular and the catalytic converter, which in 1992 became mandatory for all new cars in Britain. In the following four years, deaths by car exhaust poisoning (classified as poisoning by other gases and vapours) dropped among men by a recorded 37%. The President of the Royal College of Psychiatrists at the time, Dr Robert Kendall, observed that the introduction of catalytic converters had decreased the number of suicides without substitution of other methods.[5]

High Risk Occupational Groups in England and Wales

Occupational Groups 1988-92	PMR[*] Suicide risk (%)	Number of Suicides
Men aged 16-64		
Vets	361	18
Pharmacists	199	18
Dental Practitioners	194	18
Chemical Scientists / Engineers	156	38
Forestry Workers	155	27
University Academic Staff	152	27
Farmers	145	177
Medical Practitioners	144	60
Women aged 16-59		
Ambulance Women	402	3
Vets	387	3
Government Inspectors	365	3

Medical Practitioners	322	25
Nurses	154	247
Pharmacists	141	4
Literary / Artistic Professions	112	42

[*] PMR means Proportional Mortality Rate, a measure of suicide risk. The average for men aged 16-64 and for women aged 16-59 = 100. Thus a PMR of 365 for female Government Inspectors indicates that this group is at 3.65 times the risk of suicide as the average woman between 16 and 59.[3]

The suicide risk among male farmers decreased over the ten years 1982-92 but remained high, accounting for 1% of all male suicides during that period. Farmers and their wives averaged one a week. The availability of firearms may have been an exacerbating factor, with 38% of male farmers using this method compared to 5% of all male suicides. The wives also used firearms in 10% of their efforts to kill themselves as opposed to 1% of all female suicides. Modern farming remains a potentially lonely occupation for those who do not immerse themselves in the community in other ways. It would be remarkable if the trend does not increase again in view of the continuing crises associated with genetic engineering, the side effects of chemicals, globalisation and the mechanisation of tasks previously undertaken by many people working on the land. The glimmer of hope is that if organic farming starts belatedly to be seriously supported by government, retailers and consumers, farming will incidentally become not only better for environmental and human health, but also more labour intensive and thus less isolated.

The availability of the means to commit suicide is also illustrated among those who take their own lives in the health care professions, choosing self-poisoning to a larger degree than in the population as a whole. Nurses, for example, accounted for 5% of all female suicides during the years 1982-92.

People undergoing difficulties in their lives outside work are vulnerable to being steered towards the suicide option by insensitivity at work.

George had taught at a leading private secondary school for 15 years, but his teaching had become an increasing struggle over the past year. During that time he had had two major operations, despite which he was in almost continuous pain. At the inquest, his widow said: 'He had no doubt that he would continue, until he was summoned to a meeting in which he was given an ultimatum. He had three weeks to improve his teaching, which he had not previously been made aware of, otherwise he would be required to leave. He came out of that meeting feeling his integrity, which was unquestionable, had been questioned and he felt undermined and humiliated'. A few days later he killed himself, having written two notes, one to the school chaplain and the other to the Headteacher. The school declined to comment at the Inquest.

Suicide can also be triggered by a potentially lethal combination of organisational change combined with what is sometimes called 'macho management'. Typically the latter is a form of bullying in which a manager abuses the power that he has to threaten and intimidate his staff without concern for the pressures they may be under at or indeed outside work. One such example came with the threat of redundancy.

A large company was going through some radical change, involving a plan to 'down size' or reduce staff numbers by nearly 50%. One of the managers, Tom, had witnessed a new senior manager, who knew none of his people, come in and deliver a threatening pep talk, in which he promised them that at least half of them would be gone by the end of the year and it was up to them to demonstrate that they were worth keeping and better than the others. Shortly after that talk, one of his long standing engineers, excellent at his work but not overly self confident, disappeared. It fell to Tom after a 24 hour search to find his body. It was in his car, on one of the more distant of their scattered sites: he had shot himself through the head. Tom who knew and liked the engineer had never witnessed a sight as distressing before in his life. The tragedy was traumatic for Tom on many levels. Fortunately he had some debriefing in the psychology department of the local hospital at the firm and insistent instigation of an enlightened full time trades union official, who became involved. Tom's own line manager had not recommended that he have any support, and appeared to be oblivious to the possible need for it. To rub salt into an already very raw wound, his main concern was that Tom keep the matter away from the media.

There was widespread concern among Tom and some of his fellow middle managers that a number of newly appointed senior managers were adopting a macho style incompatible with the values and approach to managing change which underpinned what the company was officially and publicly advocating. This was one of a number of incidents which reinforced the concern that such a style can put some insecure staff, with significant financial responsibilities, under the kind of unnecessary added stress, which may be the thin edge of the suicide wedge.

Bullying at Work

Bullying, harassment or ridicule occurs at work, sometimes to the point where for a particularly vulnerable person with low self esteem, it can become unbearable. There is inevitably a fine line between firm management and bullying, but that distinction is being increasingly recognised and acknowledged.[5],[6],[7]

Bullying comes in many forms, but may include any combination of the following:

- public humiliation;
- constant negative criticism without any balancing encouragement or respect;
- shouting, sarcasm and/or sneering;
- threats of discipline, dismissal or demotion;
- unrealistic deadlines, doomed to failure;
- vague, incompetent, unclear instructions;
- lack of regard for the person's life outside work;
- arbitrary refusal for leave, time off, going home on time;
- diminishing the person or their job;
- consistently dismissing their ideas and suggestions;
- blocking promotion or training opportunities;
- negative appraisals;
- sexist, racist, ageist or homophobic behaviour;
- sneering at or attacking the person's religious, political or other beliefs or values;
- sneering at or mocking the person's appearance, accent or family
- physical intimidation.[7],[8]

Young People at Risk

Suicide accounts for 20% of all deaths among young people and is the second most common cause of death among young men, claiming more lives than cancer.[5]

Research summarised in a 1997 Samaritans report[6] indicated that the rate of suicide attempts by young men had doubled in 10 years, although subsequently it appeared to level off, but is still much higher than it used to be. Work, unemployment and study issues were contributing factors nearly twice as often with that age group as among all adults attempting suicide. 56% of young men who had attempted suicide had such problems. They were only exceeded as a possible trigger by relationship problems with a partner or another family member. Work, unemployment and study were way ahead of such difficulties as those concerning friendships, money, housing, alcohol, drugs, social isolation or psychiatric illness.

Bullying can impact particularly hard on younger people, and they are especially at risk to it. Such behaviour is disproportionately targeted at younger and newer employees. It may also be more effectively managed by some older people, whose coping strategies have been developed over time. At a younger age, some of those same people may not have built the necessary confidence, perspective and skills to contain, combat or in some way deal with bullying.. Consequently it can be magnified to the point where the person comes to believe that the only option left is to kill themselves. Among this age group, the quality of the parental relationship is an important factor: research indicates that young suicide 'attempters' report less perceived support and understanding than other adolescents who are depressed.[6]

For such youngsters, a good manager, team leader or supervisor may have some of the characteristics of a good parent, an adult role model, who is perceived to be on his or her side, firm but fair but also above all encouraging. The same effect can come through a good teacher, although large class sizes make that difficult, whereas a reasonably sized span of control at work makes a human and humane working relationship possible, if the culture reinforces it. In addition, reviving apprentice schemes or developing mentoring for young employees are additional ways of reducing the risk of depression or despair getting out of hand for this age group.

Suicide, Work, Unemployment and Men

In a study on trends in suicide and unemployment in Scotland 1976-86, a period during which there was a national increase in suicides among men of 50%, an association between the two was found among men nationally, though not among women.[9] Because this was not consistent regionally, a rise in unemployment may not be a direct cause of the large rises in suicide rates. Unemployment can be isolating, especially when individuals are picked off, but it can also be a cause of solidarity with others. As redundancy becomes more common, the stigma lessens, especially for those who find new employment or start on a self-employment route relatively quickly. Nevertheless, the financial pressures on families associated with unemployment can create a bitter cocktail of anxiety, guilt and anger among many men, not least those for whom their self esteem is tied into their success as the breadwinner.

Unemployment among older people can cut both ways. For some it is not so bad. Their children, if they had any, are beginning to be self supporting, the mortgage is paid off and the redundancy or early retirement package means that the financial pressures are not too onerous. It can be an opportunity to do something different with their life after years struggling with the daily or nightly round of toil. For others, whose self esteem and social contact was tied up with their job, its status and trappings, the experience can be devastating. The relative lack of money can make it worse, because the financial needs of an expensive family may still be considerable or because their life style was inexorably tied into conspicuous consumption. The need for another comparable job may feel urgent, and being apparently too old to be employed embittering. The scrap heap is a common metaphor for an unhappy middle age, let alone old age, for too many in a society obsessed by youth without a balancing regard for the wisdom of experience and 'the elders'.

In general men are more at risk than women (75% of suicides are by men), although there is a marked exception among young women between the ages of 15 and 19.

Suicide and Money

Suicide always involves an inquest in England and Wales, with a slightly different procedure in Scotland, which often delays the funeral. Life insurance policies frequently include a one-year suicide exclusion clause. The intention behind this is to discourage people with large debts seeing life insurance and suicide as a way of sorting out a family financial crisis. Insurance companies vary as to how rigidly they interpret such a clause. Some consider each case individually, and may use their discretion to pay out after they are satisfied that they have established all the relevant facts. Pensions are not usually affected by suicide, although some pension plans with integral life insurance may also include suicide exclusion clause.[9]

How Can I Spot Someone at Risk of Suicide?

Use what you know

Has the person you're worried about experienced any of the following:
- recent loss (a loved one, pet, job)
- the recent break-up of a close relationship
- a major disappointment (failed exams, missed job promotion)
- a change in circumstances (retirement, redundancy, children leaving home)
- physical/mental illness

Has he/she:
- made a previous suicide attempt
- a history of suicide in the family
- begun tidying up their affairs (making a will, taking out insurance)

Visual Clues

Is he/she:
- withdrawn
- low-spirited
- finding it difficult to relate to others
- taking less care of themselves
- different in some ways, for example, unusually cheerful
- tearful, or trying hard not to cry
- more irritable
- finding it hard to concentrate
- less energetic, and seems particularly tired
- eating less (or more) than usual

Things to listen for

Does he/she talk about:
- feeling suicidal (it's a myth that people who talk about it don't do it)
- seeing no hope in the future, no hope in life
- feeling worthless, a failure
- feeling very isolated and alone
- sleeping badly, especially waking early
- losing their appetite or eating more than usual

Source: The Samaritans

Signs of Suicide Risk: What Can I do?

Trust your instinct – if you're concerned, you're probably right.

Ask how the person is feeling and listen to the answer.
It's difficult to support anyone who is suicidal on your own: encourage anyone feeling low to seek emotional support, from family, friends, medical services, the Samaritans and others.

Ring the Samaritans yourself on 0345 90 90 90. We may be able to contact the person you are worried about.

Source: The Samaritans

As far as the last point is concerned, talking a concern over with either a good counsellor or the Samaritans may help you decide both what to do and, as important, how to do it.

If you suspect someone with whom you are working is feeling so low that they are contemplating suicide, should you mention it? Norman Keir, a former chairman of the Samaritans has written:

A common reason for not enquiring about suicidal feelings is the fear that to do so with someone who may be at risk could be dangerous. This is quite unfounded. Taking one's life is hardly an option one would adopt because someone had put the idea into one's head. Indeed a working party of the Royal College of General Practitioners advised that 'there should never be any hesitation in asking a depressed or agitated patient if he has wanted to kill himself'.[5]

Keir emphasises the fundamental importance of listening, which should underpin everything that is done in the name of the clinical care of the suicidal. 'On the face of it, the process of listening might seem superficial and trivial, whereas when undertaken correctly, it is one of the most potent techniques in resolving suicidal crises'.

Voluntary Euthanasia or Assisted Suicide

The debate about voluntary euthanasia continues, even while it is illegal in most countries. To seek help, especially that of a doctor, in committing suicide is based on the sense that people should have a 'right to die' or rather 'individual control, as far as is possible, of the process of dying'.[6] One study suggested that as many as a quarter of the 3,696 people interviewed would have preferred an earlier death in certain cases, rising to 35% in those over 85%, so the issue is of concern to large numbers of people in one way or another:

- 28% of respondents and 24% of the deceased had expressed a view that an earlier death would have been preferable;
- 35% of the over-85s, compared to 20% of younger people, said that they wished they had died earlier;
- only 3.6% of those who had died were said to have asked for euthanasia.
- religious faith, social class and place of residence had little bearing on people's views about euthanasia;
- people who had experienced hospice care were, if anything, more likely than others to express the view that it would have been better to have died earlier;
- fear of becoming dependent was a greater factor than pain among those expressing these wishes, although cancer patients were more likely to be motivated by pain.

Euthanasia is seen by its advocates as a means of securing a chosen, gentle, relatively easy, dignified and timely death for some otherwise condemned to die long after an acceptable quality of life has ceased.

The opposition to euthanasia is based primarily on some combination of three arguments. The first is that it is unnecessary, the second that it is open to serious abuse and the third that it is morally wrong. There have been great advances in pain relief, although the standard of knowledge in this area is more reliably and consistently spread within the hospices and among specialist doctors and nurses, including Macmillan nurses, than among doctors and hospitals in general. Enlightened and skilful doctors will not 'officiously strive' to keep a patient alive, irrespective of the quality of life or the pain that the patient may be in. Many GPs admit to using opiates to shorten life. Nevertheless, even in hospices, there may be patients who desire to end it all, but not be able to do so. One condition that has evoked such a desire among some patients is motor-neurone disease.

Advances in medicine, especially in the field of pain control, have been used to argue that euthanasia is not needed in the world of today.

Martin was an engineer in a large food production company. His young wife, Rosemary, had suffered from a debilitating and terminal form of cancer for six years, and had reached the point where there was no more treatment available at a time before the hospice movement had got going in his part of the country. For some time Rosemary, knowing that her death was getting nearer, had indicated that she wanted to die in her own home, and not go back into hospital. Her doctor, on being pressed by her, had acknowledged that after chemo and radiotherapy and many operations, they had reached the point where no more active treatment was possible and death was fairly imminent. At that time barbiturates were commonly prescribed as sleeping tablets and Rosemary had collected a supply over the months. One night she had a recurrence of severe pain, which would have meant that in the morning she would need to be readmitted to hospital. So she asked for her husband's agreement that she should take the tablets. Not wanting her to suffer any more, Martin agreed and a little later held the tablets for her while she held a glass of water from which she sipped and took them one by one, before falling into a coma. She died peacefully without regaining consciousness the next day.

Martin's grieving was complicated by the knowledge that, even though he felt that he had done what was right by Rosemary, if the way she had died had become public knowledge, he might be prosecuted for manslaughter. He was fortunate in that he was able to share the truth of her death in confidence and without guilt with a counsellor with whom he was put into contact by an enlightened manager. Keeping such a secret to himself would have increased the level of stress that had built up during his wife's illness and after her death. This was caused by trying to support his wife, to ensure that their young children were adequately cared for when she was in hospital and to maintain his effectiveness at work over an extended period.

The fear of abuse in voluntary euthanasia is both political and personal. In Germany and Europe, the Nazis, under Adolph Hitler, pursued murder under the guise of involuntary euthanasia as an instrument of policy towards whole groups of people, until their military defeat in 1945. The more personal fear is that ruthless relatives, after the money of a sick person, may prevail upon them to opt for euthanasia. Alternatively a sick, disabled or elderly person may opt for it because they do not want to be a trouble or in the way of other people.

The moral argument is similar to that which used to be deployed so widely against suicide. Life is sacred. We have no right to determine when a person dies: 'thou shalt not kill'. It has been pointed out, however, that what this Commandment delivered by Moses meant was that a Jew must not murder a Jew, but that when it came to dealing with their enemies, different criteria applied. The Egyptians found this to their cost when they tried chasing the people of Israel through the Red Sea (Exodus 14).

In addition to Holland, another modern government has tried to thread its way through this tangle by giving circumscribed rights for voluntary euthanasia to the terminally ill. The Rights of the Terminally Ill Act came into effect in Australia's Northern Territory in July 1996.[2]

Rights of the Terminally Ill Act 1995
Legislative Assembly of the Northern Territory

- The Act confirms the right of a terminally ill person to request assistance from a medically qualified person to voluntarily terminate his or her life in a humane manner.
- The patient must be over 18 and terminally ill.
- Assistance may be by administering appropriate drugs or supplying them for the patient to self-administer.
- The illness must be causing severe pain/suffering.
- The patient must not be suffering from treatable depression (an independent psychologist must confirm this).
- The doctor must share the same first language as the patient or have an accredited translator present.
- The patient must be offered and must positively refuse all further palliative care.
- There must be a period for reflection between the first discussions and the final decision.
- The doctor must be present until the patient has died.
- Insurance will not be affected.
- Foreigners will not be able to travel to Australia to benefit by the Act. (Immigration laws bar visitors in poor health)[7]

A 1999 court ruling in Britain found a GP not guilty of murder after he had admitted prescribing opiates to a terminally ill patient in order that suffering be relieved in a quantity that he knew would also bring about death.

In a Dutch study[8] of 'different exits', the majority of deaths are those where no end-of-life decisions were made: people just died, but they identified five other headings. Two were familiar: nearly 20% died from administering pain-killers in large doses and about the same proportion of people died from the decision to forgo treatment. In most of these cases doctors estimated that life had been shortened by less than a week, with patients hopefully being spared a week of misery. The other three categories are of voluntary euthanasia (about 2%) with rather less for doctor assisted suicide and the alarming category of the intentional ending of life without the patient's request: 'It could have taken another week before she died. I just needed the bed'. In a 1997 Leader,[9] the *Economist* observed that 'It would take an extraordinary law that could disentangle, in every case, the motives of mercy from those of easy disposal'. Nevertheless, the Leader concluded that it would be an abdication of moral duty if human beings did not at least make the attempt to produce such a law. Before embracing such a law, however, doctors and politicians should consider other ways to shore up the dignity and self-determination of the individual. Their list is a useful checklist of what most of us would want for each other, whether as colleagues, friends or family:

- patients should be fully informed about what is being done to them.
- patients should receive the best care possible, including palliative treatment, that is often scandalously neglected.
- patients should be able to determine where they die, at home, in a hospice or in hospital.
- patients should have the right to refuse medical treatment, either at the time or through advance directives such as 'Living Wills'.

A Living Will or Advance Directive[10] is a form expressing the individual's wish to his or her doctor but does not ask the doctor to do anything against the law. It usually asks that the following applies if the person suffers from one of a list of conditions and becomes unable to participate effectively in decisions about their medical care:

In the event of two independent physicians (one a consultant) being of the opinion that there is no reasonable prospect of recovery from serious illness or impairment involving severe distress or incapacity for rational existence:
   1. that I am not subjected to any medical intervention or treatment aimed at prolonging or sustaining my life;
   2. that any distressing symptoms (including any caused by lack of food or fluid) are to be fully controlled by appropriate analgesic or other treatment, even though that treatment may shorten my life.

The debate will continue as people consider living wills and talk among themselves and with their doctors. Whether (and if so how) a doctor should help a patient to let go of life remains a private matter between the two of them and, perhaps, their next-of-kin, within the boundaries set by the law and personal and medical ethics.

Notes

1. Alison Wertheimer *A Special Scar* (1991 Routledge, London).

2. Davies, Jean (foreword by Dirk Bogarde), *Choice in Dying: The Facts about Voluntary Euthanasia* (Ward Lock, London, 1997).

3. The Samaritans, *The Cost of Stress*, (The Samaritans 10 The Grove, Slough, SL1 1QP, 1996).

4. Ibid.

5. Keir, Norman *Suicide and Counselling* (CEPEC, London, *Insight* 3, March 1995).

6. Laurance, Jeremy 'Why Suicide Rates in Men are Dropping', (*The Independent*, London, November 1998).

7. Welsby, Ken, Survivor's Lament (*Independent on Sunday*, London, 30 June 1996).

8. The Samaritans *Challenging the Taboo: Attitudes towards Suicide and Depression*, (The Samaritans).

9. Leading Article 'The Right to Choose to Die' (*The Economist*, London, 21st June 1997).

10. The Advance Directive: information is available from The Voluntary Euthanasia Society, 13 Prince of Wales Terrace, London W8 5PG (0207 937 7770).

15

Funerals and Rites of Passage

- Deciding what to Do with the Body: Cremation or Burial?
- Checklist for Support over the Funeral from the Company:
- The Purposes of the 'Rites of Passage'
- Offering the Body for Medical Education or Research
- Cremation
- Greener Funerals
- Funeral Costs
- The Funeral
- A Service or Meeting of Thanksgiving

Deciding what to Do with the Body: Cremation or Burial?

Twentieth century population growth and technology contribute indirectly to the unfamiliarity of death. A funeral used to be held in a local church, in the churchyard of which the body would then be buried. People went to the same place for rituals surrounding birth, marriage and death. Thus symbolically in the midst of life we encounter death and vice versa. And since, for many, the church was part of weekly, if not daily, life, it was easier to sense (with William Blake) that:

> Joy and Woe are woven fine,
> A clothing for the soule divine.
> Under every grief and pine
> Runs a joy with silken twine.

When the churchyards started to fill up, cremation became the solution to overcrowding, especially in densely populated urban areas. The Cremation Society was formed in England in 1885 and the last opposition to cremations was removed in 1964 with the lifting of the Vatican's ban on the practice. It is now in Britain the main way of disposing of a body, with an estimated

71% of funerals involving it; although this figure is proportionately lower in Scotland than in the more crowded countries of England and Wales.[1] While there may be much to recommend cremation, it led to the development of places associated only with death. In crematoria, death is separated from the rest of life – an unconscious and unintended expression of our contemporary enthusiasm for specialisation.

Behaviour is strongly influenced by culture. The cluster of attitudes which underlie the rituals described above is now being steadily questioned. In the multi-cultural society of late 20th century Britain we are beginning to realise that other traditions have helpful ways of responding to death which do not minimise it. Cultures are never static and there are signs that the British one is becoming more open and flexible. There is a more widespread sense than there used to be that people need to do it 'their way' and be respected for doing so. Notes on some of the beliefs and customs around death of some of the main religious and irreligious traditions in Britain form part of the next chapter, 16.

When a member of staff dies, whether they were still working or retired, colleagues who knew them are usually very welcome at the 'Rites of Passage'. By going, the dead person is being honoured and their family supported. Sometimes several colleagues going, especially if the person has worked for a long time for the same organisation, can be especially valued. The weight of numbers of people coming to a funeral is often noticed and a source of comfort to the close family. It is as if the regard for the person who has died is being affirmed by the numbers of people from the community, including the workplace, who give up their time to come. A book or card, which those attending sign, can reinforce that afterwards, as the next-of-kin may be hardly aware of who else is there.

Letters and donations to a nominated charity (or flowers) can reinforce that same message. Among the colleagues may be the line manager and/or the most senior director or executive in the organisation who knew the person who has died. Their attendance can have a powerful representative role, particularly if the senior person has a deserved reputation for behaving with integrity and for being caring.

In the same way, a representative or two from the company can also be supportive to a staff member at a 'rite of passage' for one of their particularly close relatives, such as a parent or child.

Often the members of staff will organise the event without needing help from their workplace and will indicate, one way or another, whether work colleagues are welcome. There are times when this is not the case if the boss or company, through the stress it put the staff member under, is thought to have contributed to a premature death. If in doubt, give permission and encouragement to others close to the person to attend.

Checklist for Support over the Funeral from the Company

Offer, via the line manager, a Human Resources person or other suitable company representative, contact before the funeral, if possible with a visit to establish any or all of the following:

- Does the next-of-kin need support for planning what to do immediately?
- Do they need money urgently to help pay for expenses?
- What are the wishes of the deceased or immediate family?
- Would they like a book from the company for attenders at the funeral to sign (if so, keep the company aspect low key in the book)?
- Any other ways in which the company could help?

Consider the following issues as well:

- Who at work needs to be informed (and how) and who might attend the funeral?
- Time off to be arranged sensitively.
- Any transport implications?
- Anyone whom the next-of-kin particularly want (or do not want) to attend?
- A personally signed letter from the most senior person appropriate to the next-of-kin, expressing appreciation of the deceased as well as condolences.
- A donation to the specified charity or flowers to be sent: if flowers, do not make them ostentatious so that that they do not dwarf those from close family or friends.

In many cases, colleagues will of course themselves have a personal relationship and friendship with the partner or child who has died, especially where the gap between work and home is not too rigidly defined. There is often a difference between work located in cities and those in smaller towns or villages. People commute, for example, from far and wide to central

London jobs, making it less likely that they would see colleagues outside work.

In certain occupations, particularly for a death in service, the organisation of a 'rite of passage' may be undertaken by the employee in consultation with the next-of-kin. Examples of this include the armed forces, police, fire and ambulance services and the churches. In other situations, the dying person or the next-of-kin, may feel uncertain about what to do about rites of passage. In the rest of this chapter, the aim is to help such a person decide what to do (or to help their manager guide them towards appropriate decisions).

The Purposes of the 'Rites of Passage'

Although there are many variations, the themes of 'rites of passage' in different cultures tend towards meeting the five basic needs to:

1) Do something appropriate with the dead body relatively quickly before decomposition makes it an added source of distress and offence.
2) Say farewell to the person, at least in their existence and their body in this life, whether or not their death is regarded as the end, and perhaps also to help the dead person's spirit on to the next phase of their existence.
3) Honour and celebrate the person who has died.
4) Acknowledge and begin to come to terms with the reality of the death.
5) Provide a focal point for collective grieving and comfort for supporting those people who are grieving the most.

The Rites of Passage commonly used in Europe can be used in various combinations. They are discussed below, but in summary are:

- a funeral at which the body is present in a coffin, typically, but not necessarily in a place of worship. This may be in the form of a Requiem Mass or Communion service.
- the farewell to the body, often with a short service and commendation, at a crematorium or by the graveside straight after the funeral.
- In the case of cremation, the ashes may be subsequently buried or scattered either in the crematorium or in a special place.
- a Service of Thanksgiving or a non-religious Thanksgiving Meeting or Gathering, which may be held some time after the

funeral in almost any location. In the past, this event tended to be called a Memorial Service.

A variation on the last of these is to hold a short service to say farewell to the person and for the disposal of the body, followed by a Service or Meeting of Thanksgiving, an event in which the person and his or her life can be celebrated.

The social get-together after the funeral is as important in its own way. The mourners can talk and reminisce about the deceased and reconnect with each other. It can be based in the home or a more neutral setting, such as a community or church hall or a hotel. A possible disadvantage of the home is the pressure on those most affected to stay until the end, rather than have a place to which they can retreat, if they feel the need.

Offering the Body for Medical Education or Research

The first decision to make is what to do with the body? Cremated or buried are the options in Britain, with an interim possibility that it or part of it be offered for medical education or research or for transplant surgery.

A body can be offered in the will or by the next-of-kin after someone has died to be used in the training of doctors or more rarely for medical research. Generally badly diseased bodies will not be suitable, so be prepared for the offer to be turned down for this or some other reason. If the body is accepted, the remains will normally be returned, perhaps a year later, for disposal. This needs to be prepared and planned for, so that the next-of-kin is given good support, whatever the decision.

Cremation

The next decision to take is what combination of Rites of Passage? This might be either for myself when my time comes or for my next-of-kin who has died – or is just about to die? The minimal option is a cremation service, which will be often restricted to 20 minutes or so, unless a double slot is booked.

If the body is to be cremated, the question follows: what to do with the ashes? Arrangements can be made for them to be buried in a crematorium garden, churchyard or scattered in a chosen place. Ashes are bio-degradable and are soon absorbed into land or sea. They can be scattered or buried straight into the earth or buried in an urn, or container, which will – at least for a time – protect them from being absorbed back into the earth.

There are four options for the crematorium chapel. The first is to ask someone to take the service, such as your local minister, priest, rabbi or a friend; the second, for it to be taken by the local clergyman who may be on duty that day. The third is for you to take it yourself as next-of-kin. Lastly you have the choice of no service at all. One problem with a Crematorium-only funeral is that the time is usually severely restricted and it can be hard to avoid it feeling hurried or perfunctory. On the other hand, that time is fine for some people.

Crematorium chapels can often also be restricted in space. It has been known for half the congregation in a well-attended funeral to be unable to get in, gathering around the door straining to hear. The ashes are usually available later the same day or the following day to be buried or scattered.

Greener Funerals

Increasingly a green approach to death is raising questions about the burning of coffins. Alternative approaches may become more common in future. These already, for example, include the burning of the body in a body bag allowing the coffin to be passed on or otherwise reused or the use of cheap, biodegradable coffins made from cardboard or other material.

For the environmentally conscious, burials are sometimes now taking place in woods with a commemorative tree planted over the burial place. The Bishop of Coventry, for example, consecrated a woodland burial site for such a purpose in Coventry in 1995. The wood is not just a place of death, but a living and beautiful place. The tree represents new life coming from the old, a symbolism accessible to the agnostic or religious person.

Funeral Costs

Even cheaper funerals have been costed at about £700 in the UK, and £1000 is normal, whereas across the English Channel the cost can be a great deal less. At 1999 prices, the basic costs of the funeral director with a relatively cheap wooden coffin, caring for the body until the funeral and a hearse to take the coffin to the funeral can come to about £750. Hard wood coffins are much more expensive in financial as well as environmental terms. The hire of extra cars to carry mourners a further £70 each, church and clergy £75, with an organist £30 extra, doctors' fees for cremation certificates £80 and the fee to the crematorium £200.

The Funeral

A funeral is often led by a minister of religion: an estimated 70% of funerals taking place in England are conducted by Church of England clergy. The Church's General Synod has discussed the degree of preparation and support given to the bereaved through these processes. Sometimes this is exemplary with sensitive pastoral care and a service that honours the person who has died. Sadly some funerals in crematoria can appear to be impersonal and peremptory. It can be difficult for the priest or minister if there has been no previous contact with the deceased or their family or friends.

There are the clergy from hell or even well meaning ones who are crassly insensitive. 'The vicar stood to make a sermon. The exposition was lengthy ... We were told how Jesus was our friend, and why Christianity was different from all other religions, being more than a set of rules. There was no reference to the life we were celebrating, or even to the reason why we were there ... As the sermon took its course, the temperature in the congregation seemed to drop by about 10 degrees'.[2]

While the idea of a painless funeral may be over-optimistic, a well prepared and sensitively conducted funeral can and often does bring more comfort than distress, even though it may have been dreaded in anticipation. This ceremony needs to be well done in order that the person to whom people are bidding farewell is honoured through it. This is exemplified by a poem read at the funeral of a friend, Tom Kinsey. In death we are all equal in the sight of God or of at least enlightened men and women:

> Not how did he die, but how did he live?
> Not what did he gain, but what did he give?
> These are the units to measure the worth
> Of a man as a man, regardless of birth.
>
> Not what was his church, nor what was his creed?
> But had he befriended those really in need?
> Was he ever ready with word of good cheer,
> To bring back a smile and to banish a tear?
> Not what did the words in the obituary column say,
> But who was sorry when he passed away.

To ensure that it is neither rushed nor overcrowded, a service or meeting in a church, other place of worship or in a secular building needs to be planned to include as many as want to come, say 100 or more people for a reasonable length of time, say, between 45 to 60 minutes. That leaves an option for a smaller number of people to go on to the crematorium for the service there, usually immediately afterwards or a little later that day. Where crematoria are far from the place of worship, an alternative option is to have the service there first and then a service or meeting, as a form of Thanksgiving perhaps, afterwards. This logistically may be the only way of allowing the mourners to meet socially together after the funeral, which may be an important part of the whole process.

We live in a period of unprecedented diversity in what people believe or do not believe, and in religious and non-religious allegiances. This means that there are also correspondingly more choices about where to hold a funeral, who to involve and what to include.

> George, a computer programmer, died young and his widow wanted a service for him that honoured who he was. He was an agnostic Stoic, with a deep love of music. She was a Roman Catholic and they also had many Jewish friends. The funeral was planned to reflect both the integrity of his scepticism and also beliefs implicit in the other two traditions so that the people who came could all feel that the service was appropriate for them. It took place in the local Roman Catholic church, whose priest co-operated fully in supporting the people who took part, including a Church of England minister. Prayers were prayed to God rather than through Jesus, and it was noted that the Lord's Prayer of Jesus was originally a Jewish as well as subsequently a 'Christian' prayer. The word God can be given a personal meaning by each individual, as the focal point of what they most honour – whether it is the Creator of the Universe, the Spirit of Music or the love and justice that exists among people at their best. A musical improvisation by a double bass playing, sailing friend of George was an especially moving tribute transcending verbal language, which can so easily tie us up in conflicting knots. Expressing and valuing such diversity of belief as a healthy reality can dispel a sense of hypocrisy and bring people together in a genuine unity, which is particularly needed at a funeral.

This sense of not so much burying our differences as living in peace together in a period of grieving is sometimes experienced in public as well as private life. In recent years, this happened when John Smith, the British Labour Party leader, died. Tributes were paid to him by opponents, as well as allies, very different in tone from the adversarial insults so often traded in the House of Commons. In the face of death, so often our squabbles seem petty all of a sudden and our differences, which can inspire such passion on other days, trivial.

The next question is the extent you take such a service 'off the shelf' so to speak or make your own input. Your request to do the latter may be resisted and there are still clergy who expect to have the final say on every detail, but thankfully they are a decreasing minority. Most people taking funerals will welcome suggestions for hymns, other music, prayers, readings and offers of help to play or speak, so that the service really reflects the person who has died. Some might raise an eyebrow at the funeral of a friend, which began on his instructions with 'There's no business like show business' setting the tone for a service which was authentic and moving, evoking laughter as well as tears, which was of course his intention all along.

Some people plan their own funeral down to the last detail and find comfort in doing so. It can also help the next-of-kin with their decision making over the rites of passage. Others neither want nor feel able to do this while they are alive, but may tell a close friend or family member a few items they would like included. Otherwise the person closest to them may, discreetly or otherwise depending on their relationship, make their own notes of favourite poems, music, readings or hymns. It will then be left to the next-of-kin to make the actual arrangements after the person has died. Some clergy, like funeral directors, are more open to suggestions than others.

When David's father died, he had to cope with an undertaker who was not a skilled listener and tried to tell him and his family what was proper. It turned out to be something of a struggle with her, which was very difficult at such a vulnerable time. Nevertheless, they ended up getting mostly what they wanted. This included his father's embalmed body staying in his home for six days until the funeral, allowing members of the extended family to make their own farewells in their own time and in their own way. It would not suit many people, but it worked well for them. Then the evening before the funeral, his father's body in its coffin was taken to the church. It remained there overnight, with members of the family taking turns to keep vigil with it.

When David's mother died, on the other hand, a very different funeral director concentrated on understanding and implementing the wishes of the family. So when they wanted four younger members of the family to carry her coffin into and out of the church, he agreed readily – only asking to meet them briefly to instruct them on the best way to lift, carry and lower the coffin, so that no mishap occurred.

A Service or Meeting of Thanksgiving

A service of thanksgiving to celebrate the life of the person as well as mourn their passing, separately from and after the funeral, takes place for a minority of people but it can also be helpful. Until relatively recently, the phrase Memorial Service was common, although it is a 20th century phenomenon, with the Memorial Service for Queen Victoria marking the beginning of what soon came to be a tradition for the famous or publicly distinguished. A Requiem Mass honours the person too, but its purpose is also to pray for their soul in its onward journey through purgatory and, hopefully, onward to heaven, being with God.

At the beginning of the 21st century the memorial service has been largely replaced by the idea of a service or meeting of thanksgiving. The positive element in this is the celebration of a person's life, with grief implied but largely under the surface. It can even reflect the bereavement process if the funeral occurs soon after the person has died, when grief is raw, even if mixed with shock and denial. That service needs in particular to avoid the tyranny of the positive in which pretence and the stiff upper lip rule supreme. There needs to be some acknowledgement in both the funeral and Thanksgiving of loss and sadness towards the positive, reflecting to an extent the hoped for movement through some of the worst and most acute grief. It can be like a marker of the end of the period of formal mourning, even though that may not be either intended or expressed in most British cultures. That balance is captured by C.S. Lewis when he wrote that 'the pain now is part of the happiness then'. Memory in the ritual of memorial can recall all that was good and loveable about the person, which is the raw material of why their loss is the subject of sadness.

Such an event tends to be work orientated for those who have a public as well as a private life. Alternatively it may take place in a different place than the funeral, where the person who died has strong associations. John Smith's funeral was in Scotland, while his service of thanksgiving took place in Westminster Abbey, across the road from where he worked. The company may consequently offer to take a lead in organising a Service for and on behalf of the family in a way which would seldom be appropriate with the funeral. Alternatively the offer might be to assist in such a way that the next-of-kin does not feel marginalised.

Whether it's a meeting or a service depends on what auspices it comes under. Humanists and those who do not think of themselves as religious may plump for a meeting in a secular setting. Quakers also use the term meeting as well, while a service implies a religious dimension, albeit in a gathering of diverse views and beliefs, the common currency of contemporary society.

Notes

1. Christian, K. *Handbook of Religious Trends* 1998 (Paternoster Publishing, Carlisle, London 1997).
2. *The Guardian*, 19 November 1998.

16

Culture, Religion and Death

- The Influences of Culture on Our Response to Death
- Religion and Death
- Spiritual Support
- Some of the Main Religious and Atheist Approaches:
  - Buddhism
  - Christianity
  - Hinduism
  - Humanism
  - Islam
  - Judaism
  - Sikh Religion
- Working with Your Own Experiences

The Influences of Culture on Our Response to Death

Different religions have developed in different human societies, but often there are striking common themes. With their ceremonies and mythology, they are superficially so different that it has been easy to exaggerate their deeper differences, especially if politically they were being used as a mask for competition and military conquest. As we strive for religions to be vehicles for peace, not war, we discover similar values and myths being worked and reworked, finding expression in different cultures.

Religions and philosophical systems, like Stoicism, which are not thought of as religions, serve a variety of purposes, such as providing people with a common language and value system. They can provide an explanation for the mysteries of our existence and help us, individually and collectively, to develop a moral basis and a sense of purpose for our lives. The language of religion at its most powerful is poetry, mythology, music, art and architecture, rather than prose. All of these provide the raw material for the rituals surrounding dying and death and our attempts to communicate about and make sense of them.

Religion can provide us with a sense of perspective, such as the Biblical invocation from the Book of Ecclesiastes, chapter 3, verses 1 - 4:

> For everything its season,
> and for every activity under heaven its time:
> a time to be born and a time to die;
> a time to plant and a time to uproot;
> a time to kill and a time to heal;
> a time to pull down and a time to build up;
> a time to weep and a time to laugh;
> a time for mourning and a time for dancing.

Or express the need for hope within despair and poverty, as in the Christian Aid prayer:

> Though what is past
> may be full of loss
> and the present insecure,
> never shall despair
> take away our future.
>
> Give us the seeds of hope, O God,
> and we will clear the ground,
> plant and weed, and work and laugh,
> our harvest safe in your hands.

Religion and Death

Through religion, human beings have speculated widely about what, if anything, might happen after death. Religious faith stretches the mind to its limits as we struggle to imagine the unimaginable: our possible survival outside the dimensions of time and space after our body (including our brain) has been destroyed. Some people believe that we survive individually in a kind of ethereal non-physical body; others that the soul survives in a disembodied form; others again that we are reincarnated in another body; and others that we are absorbed into unity with all matter, losing any sense of our own individuality. Yet others remain convinced that death is unequivocally the end of everything.

Many are clear only about their uncertainty: death is surrounded in mystery. As psychical research, physics, psychology and theology wrestle with the issue in different ways, the destiny for many is to die in doubt about life after death. For them, reflection leads to the refining of hope rather than belief.

On the other hand, many other people approach death confident that it is the gateway to something unimaginably positive and wonderful. C.S. Lewis[1] described it at the end of his Narnia stories for children of all ages: 'All their life in this world and all their adventures in Narnia had only been the cover and the title page: now at last they were beginning Chapter One of the Great Story which no one on earth has read: which goes on forever: in which every chapter is better than the one before'.

> Imelda, a shop manager, had retired from the company 10 years before but kept contact through a thriving company bridge club. After a series of strokes it became clear that she was dying. She had had a frustrating life in many ways, but she approached death with great serenity and optimism. Although she had not been a regular church-goer and had no conventional belief in an afterlife, she felt that 'although I can't describe it, I know it's going to be alright'.

The sense that reality is ultimately benevolent, despite all the mixed messages of our existence, is the most hopeful response to the mystery of what may or may not come after death. Faith or no faith, death can help us to reassess our values and priorities and sort out what is really important. Dr Johnson wrote that being told that you will die in a fortnight 'wonderfully concentrates the mind'. John Brown is often quoted as saying, as he walked out to be executed in the American Civil War, that until that moment he had never fully realised how beautiful the world is.

Spiritual Support

The sense that our consciousness has a spiritual dimension, which permeates our physical, emotional and mental experience, is at the root of 'authentic religion'.[2] When death causes a sense of the spiritual to rise to the surface of our awareness, explicitly religious support is sometimes required.

Religious ritual provides a social structure for support and mourning in which the place of the spiritual is central: to express the meaning of it in prose is difficult, which is why so much religious writing can feel lifeless and empty and why we need music, art and poetry. Spiritual support can also be important on a one-to-one basis. You do not have to be a minister of religion to offer prayer for someone who is dying. It can mean a great deal to share a prayer or meditation. How it is done requires striking a balance between having the courage to offer something in a relaxed and natural way while having the restraint not to press it or spin it out unduly. It is particularly discourteous and alienating to pray with someone at their most vulnerable, if the person does not want it.

The guiding principle is to be 'person-centred'. Respect where the person is. It is no time to impose your own views. Although many find comfort in a strong belief in a life after death, others with no such belief can prepare themselves for death equally well. Indeed forms of belief which involve an expectation after death of agony in hell at the hands of the devil or a sadistic God can create an added dimension of terror. This kind of barbaric religion is increasingly under threat, even though, tragically, some still approach their own death with a dread of severe and unforgiving punishment in the afterlife.

Some of the Main Religious and Atheist Approaches

Buddhism

Buddhism sees life as a process of birth, ageing, illness and death, through which people may move towards enlightenment. We live and then we die. Whilst all physical manifestations of life must decline and disintegrate, life itself cannot be destroyed. Death is the time when a person's entity gathers energy to take on a new visible form. This continual rhythm of physical appearance, followed by death, is the very rhythm of life itself. Life after death is a form of energy, because energy is never destroyed. The energy is constant, even though our physical matter changes completely every seven years. It is the energy which gives us a sense of continuity. Death only changes the form of the energy from active to passive, not the energy itself. Death can thus be thought of as a period of latency, of passive life, just a different manifestation of life itself.

The body of a member of the family is usually kept at home for up to 3 days, when friends and relatives come to pay their respects with offerings of money or food. On the day of the funeral, the coffin is typically taken in procession to the grave and a priest or monk is often asked to come to pray for the soul of the person who has died. On each anniversary of the death, to show respect and honour to their memory, an offering of food is made on the altar in the home, dedicated to family ancestors.

Buddhism teaches that there are nine levels of consciousness: the ability to hear, see, smell, feel and taste are the first five; the 6th is our conscious mind, the 7th – abstract thought and judgement – is active when we are both awake and asleep. The 8th level is where karma is stored during life and this becomes dominant over the other 7 near to death. Our karma is every function of our lives, thoughts, words and deeds created through our other seven levels of consciousness. The 9th consciousness is the essence of universal and eternal life, which can potentially permeate the other 8 levels. After our physical death, we will remain in the state most strongly evoked in our karma, until our life becomes active again.[3]

Nirvana is an important concept in Buddhism, which means literally extinction or quenching and is the culmination of the spiritual journey for the truly enlightened person. Like the Christian idea of eternity, Nirvana is beyond, not after, death, because it is beyond or outside time and exists whether or not anyone attains it. It is the extinction of the 'fires' of attachment, hatred and delusion, and Nirvana is the resultant state, which is beyond this world in the form of birth, ageing and death.[4]

Christianity

Christians mostly believe in a life after death, but others are unsure and instead see our destination with God to be in eternity, which is both outside time and space but may be experienced in flashes of experience in the present. As God is justice as well as compassion, we are being judged for our behaviour and our thoughts in relation to our love of God and of our neighbour, including our own willingness to forgive others.

Justice requires that people who are adult at least take some responsibility for their behaviour and face up to its consequences somehow, sometime, even if they manage to escape human justice. The pattern of repentance and forgiveness, which can lead to a fresh start and a conversion from the old ways of sin, demands it.

Traditionally judgement becomes fully apparent after or at the point of our death. Heaven and hell were originally ideas from a prescientific concept of a three tier universe. God was up in heaven above the sky, hell was down below the flat earth and we

lived out our lives in the middle. For some there is an interme-
diate stage after we die, purgatory. In this we are purged of our
sinfulness to the point where we are able to cope with being in
the presence of God or not, as the case may be. Heaven would be
hell for us if we cannot cope with the inescapable goodness and
love of God.

In the 18th century many European theologians came to
doubt that there was literally such a place as hell (or heaven).
They did not rush to make this attitude public, however, since it
was thought that the fear of damnation was essential to maintain
public morality.[5] Eternity is now a concept that transcends or is
outside our time and space, and is therefore almost beyond
human imagining: it is as mysterious as God him or herself.
Some Christians construct in their minds a parallel existence, in
which time at least exists in a way, in order to make sense of what
happens when we die.

The ancient and authoritative Apostles' creed states
succinctly that 'I believe in the resurrection of the body and the
life everlasting.' Today most orthodox Christian teaching
continues to combine a belief in a life after death with that of
resurrection from the dead, although some Christians put the
emphasis of Jesus' teaching on the experience of liberation and
'new life' here and now, rather than 'pie in the sky when we die'.
Meanwhile 'it is not likely that there can emerge easily a
Christian consensus on death and the after life, at any rate for a
long time'.[6] Such a consensus is no more easily to be reached
outside Christian circles.

Outside fundamentalist circles, in which the Bible is taken to
be literally true, heaven and hell are now thought of as
metaphors or as states of being in which we either participate in
the life of or are estranged from God, from our roots. For some
Christians, heaven is inconceivable for people immediately after
death and they consequently envisage a half way house, purgatory, in which the person is enabled to be in the undiluted
presence of God. For Christians death is a time for grieving and
celebration of the person's life, and this balance is often the aim
of the funeral arrangements, which fit into the options described
earlier in this chapter.

The various historical splits between the Christian Churches, as
with splits in other religions, have had a positive as well as a
destructive element. They have enabled personal and cultural
diversity to flower in a way that might have been more difficult in

a unified church. Now that diversity is being belatedly honoured, the need for such splits as a means of the survival of religious integrity is becoming less pronounced. Hence the growth of the ecumenical movement, in which different churches and even different religions realise that what unites them is more important and that their differences are more interesting than scandalous.

Hinduism

Hindus, like Buddhists, believe in reincarnation, the nature of which is determined by the balance of good and bad deeds during our life. The souls of all living creatures are immortal. All life is sacred because God is in everything: to respect all life is to respect God. The combination of meditation, prayer and behaviour all combine to produce our Karma. Whatever evil we do comes back to us, if not in this life, in the way we are reborn. Our karma is with us through our reincarnations.

'Finite they say are these are bodies indwelt by an eternal embodied soul – a soul indestructible ... As a man casts off his worn out clothes, and takes on other new ones in their place, so does the embodied soul cast off his worn out bodies and enters another anew ... For sure is the death of all that comes to birth, sure the birth of all that dies.' (Bhagavad Gita 2:18,22,27)

The Hindu who is ill or dying will want to hear readings from the Bhagavad Gita, and may want to lie on the floor, close to Mother Earth. The family will want a Hindu priest to perform holy rites, perhaps blessing the person and sprinkling water on them from the river Ganges to help the person to accept death philosophically. His or her relatives may also bring clothes and money for him or her to touch before being passed on to the needy. Relatives are likely to accept death openly, which includes crying and expressing strong emotion. They prefer if possible to prepare the body themselves at home for the funeral, which if possible should take place within 24 hours of the death. Hindus tend to prefer cremation, although children and babies can be buried, with ashes scattered in a river, ideally the Ganges.

Humanism

'The mainsprings of moral action are what Darwin called the social instincts – those altruistic, co-operative tendencies that are as much part of our innate biological equipment as are our tendencies towards aggression and cruelty.'[7] Humanists generally want to distance themselves from belief in God, religion or a belief in an afterlife, with a focus on the human rather than the divine Spirit, and consequently want to arrange for the funeral to be free from religious input and trappings. They are often agnostic (not knowing or believing that it is possible to believe in God) or atheist (being sure that there is no God). Generally they are likely to be sceptical about the value of religion, which is essentially something educated men and women are likely to outgrow, especially if they can develop the maturity not to be dependent on the false comfort offered by religion. There are also some who feel a poignant sense of loss as they believe that they have outgrown what may have been a fine part of their lives. Radical religious people can be close to Humanists in what they believe. This can be a source of fruitful dialogue or an irritant in muddying what should be clear water between the atheist and the religious! The British Humanist Association (see Appendix 4) is a focal point for humanists and can also provide help with non-religious funerals.

Non-specifically religious rituals are also developing. One that has begun in the last decade or two is the practice in Britain of creating a shrine in memory of a person who has died tragically. Plaques have been put in the place where WPC Fletcher was shot in 1984 while on duty during the Libyan Embassy siege and where Stephen Lawrence was murdered in 1997 in an unprovoked racist attack, also in London.

Spontaneously bunches of flowers are now frequently put in public places where people have suddenly been killed, either through road accidents or murder.

Islam

There is a strong Muslim belief in a life after death, which only separates us temporarily from those we love. There are different interpretations of the detail, some thinking that the body corrupts releasing the spirit and others that the body itself takes the spirit into the afterlife. Grieving is nevertheless often intense and uninhibited. Islam means surrender and most mourners in a Muslim ceremony believe in surrendering to the will of Allah. Grieving is often unrestrained and the ceremony marked by urgency and spontaneity.

After death, the body should if possible be in the custody of Muslims. Normally only women wash a woman's body and men a man's. Any non-Muslim required to touch the body should wear disposable gloves. The body is dressed in a white shroud, called a coffin, and should be buried, as was the prophet Mohammed, within 24 hours of dying with the head facing in the direction of Mecca, the holy city of Islam. The ceremony is simple, if possible, with burial in a Muslim cemetery still usually a man's affair, although women have started to accompany the funeral procession. It is a duty for family and friends to visit the bereaved.[8]

Muslims do not practice cremation, because of a belief that the body stays in the grave until God raises everyone from death on the Last Day to be judged when people will go for eternity to heaven or to hell.

Judaism

'To everything there is a season: a time to be born, a time to die'. Judaism draws from Old Testament and rabbinical texts, although how that material is interpreted for today, as with many religions, varies between conservative or 'orthodox' and liberal or progressive movements. As with Christians and Muslims, some Jews believe in the resurrection of the dead, which is one of the 13 principles of faith set out by Maimonides. God will end when he decides to do so, creating a new world, a new Jerusalem and the Temple. Other Jews believe in a spirit world to which people go after death, rather than the idea of the Last Day.

Some Jews now choose cremation, whereas traditionally it was forbidden. The body would always be buried as soon as possible within three days of death. Coffins are simple, and undecorated, so that no differentiation is made between rich and poor. If the cemetery is fairly accessible, the service begins in the chapel, which is stark, without flowers. Donations to a designated charity is the norm. Men and women usually stand apart at the service, in which typically there will be psalms (especially Psalm 23), a memorial prayer and a eulogy.

Jewish cemeteries are called the House of Life, symbolising that death is not the end and that God will look after the faithful beyond the grave. The coffin is taken in procession, during which Psalm 91 is recited, to the grave. The men attending fill the grave with soil. The shovel should not be passed from hand to hand, but replaced each time in the soil. The procession returns to the chapel, where everyone greets the mourners, before going back to the house of mourning, often that of the deceased for a meal, prepared by others. There are customs to guide behaviour in the house of mourning, especially during the week of 'Shiva' following the funeral.

Visiting the sick is a religious duty (mitzvah) and it is important to pray and to work for the person's recovery, because of the sanctity of human life. 'Cast me not off in my old age when my strength fails, forsake me not .... But as for me, I will hope continually' (Psalm 71). Often a rabbi is wanted to help the dying person with prayer. A deathbed confession, where possible, is expected as preparation for the next stage. The Mishnah puts it: 'The world is like an antechamber to the world to come; prepare thyself in the antechamber that thou mayest enter into the hall.'

After death, the treatment of the body is seen as a religious act and rules should be observed, preferably by trained volunteers of the same sex. Desecration of the body is forbidden in the Book of Deuteronomy (chapter 21) and so post-mortems are not allowed unless the civil law requires it or if it is believed that an autopsy might save someone else.

About half the number of Jewish people in the UK, who are marrying, are choosing a gentile partner. Traditionally only Jews can be buried in a Jewish cemetery, although consideration is now beginning to be given in some liberal circles to the possibility of a couple from a mixed marriage being buried together in a Jewish cemetery.

There is little about life after death in the Old Testament, which emphasises this life. However rabbinical teaching developed a concept of the immortality of the soul and even the resurrection of the dead. Judaism is described by Jeanne Samson Katz as both this-worldly and other-worldly.[9] This paradox is illustrated by the 2nd century Rabbi Jacob: 'Better is one hour of repentance and good deeds in this world than the whole life of the world to come; yet better is one hour of blissfulness of spirit in the world to come than the whole life of this world'.

Sikh Religion

Sikhs, like Hindus, believe in reincarnation. Their life cycles depend on how they live their present life. Some Sikhs are confirmed by taking 'Amrit', after which they should attend the temple daily for prayer and wear the 5 symbols, the 'Ks': Keshas – uncut hair, Kangha – the comb, Kara – a sieel bangle, Kirpan – a short sword, and Kaachh – a pair of shorts as underwear. These symbols, especially the hair, wherever possible, should not be removed in life or after death.

A dying Sikh will be comforted by reciting hymns from the Guru Granth Sahib. If they are not well enough, this may be done by a relative, a reader from the local temple or even another practising Sikh. Relatives prefer as far as possible to be with the person as they die. The family should be asked if they wish to wash and lay out the body, although it is also usually acceptable for non-Sikhs to tend to the body. The body is normally displayed at home prior to cremation for friends and relatives to view. Sikhs are always cremated, if possible within 24 hours, and the ashes normally scattered in a river, preferably the Ganges. Funeral rites, with a procession to the crematorium, are important. When attending funerals, women usually wear a white head covering.

Working with Your Own Experience

What seems to help people come to terms with death is for them to have faith or, as it originally means, trust in the situation in which they find themselves. This may involve them trying to work out, in the light of experience, what they believe about death and come up with their own conclusions, however tentative. They may however put their trust in an existing religious or non-religious position, because they trust the people who espouse it and accept its teaching. Whether or not this takes them to a religious or an agnostic position, orthodox or unorthodox, seems secondary. The people who sometimes find it harder to cope with death are those who have repeatedly avoided the issue, as if it was too terrifying or depressing to contemplate. Their need for support may be consequently greater and the support all the more valuable, even though they may doggedly persist in denying that need.

Notes

1. Lewis, C.S. *The Four Loves* (Geoffrey Bless, London 1960).
2. Smart, N. 'Death in the Judaeo-Christian Tradition', in *Man's*

Concern with Death, A. Toynbee *et al.*, (Hodder & Stoughton, London, 1968).

3. D'Ardenne, P. and Mahtani, A. *Transcultural Counselling in Action*, (Sage, London 1989).

4. His Holiness the Dalai Lama *The Good Heart* (Rider, London 1996).

5. Parks, Colin Murray, Laungani, Pittu and Young, Bill (eds.) *Death and Bereavement across Cultures*, (Routledge, London 1996);

6. Ibid.

7. Knight, Margaret *Humanist Anthology, from Confucius to Bertrand Russell* (Barrie & Rockcliff, London 1961)

8. Collins, David, Tank, Manju and Basith, Abdul *Concise Guide to Customs of Minority Ethnic Religions*, (Portsmouth Diocesan Council for Social Responsibility, 1992).

9. Jacobs, Louis *What Does Judaism Say About?* (Keter, Jerusalem, 1973).

17

Case Studies

Death of a Colleague and a Friend

Daniel was an industrial relations manager in the motor industry. He had a deserved reputation for handling the pressure well of what at times were heated and tense negotiations about pay and conditions. But after the death of Bob, a friend who was also a colleague, Daniel became very low, finding it hard to concentrate and maintain his motivation to the point where his boss suggested it might be useful for him to see a counsellor. Daniel agreed and three strands emerged from the counselling, helping him regain his focus and energy.

Bob was a few years older than Daniel, and had been a bit of a father figure to him when he started in the company, guiding and encouraging him. Their working relationship grew into a friendship, in which they shared a passion for Aston Villa, and often a drink at the end of the day. The friendship matured into one much more of equals as Daniel grew in seniority and confidence, finding ways in which he could help Bob, especially in financial and taxation matters. But in talking about what Bob's friendship and his death had meant to him, Daniel found that the memories of how he had felt when his parents had died years before had also been stirred up. It was as if he was experiencing a double or even triple bereavement. This was particularly extreme, because he had not been able or been given the opportunity to grieve over their deaths. So he came to realise that he needed to focus on all three separately to allow the healing of his grief to happen.

Daniel's parents had separated twenty years previously, when he was 10. He and his brother lived with his mother in Bristol, losing contact with his father who moved up north with a new job. After three years, when Daniel was 13, his mother collapsed in front of him, was rushed into hospital (after he alerted a neighbour) and died a week later.

Daniel's father reappeared in order to care for the children after his wife's death. After a predictably rocky start to the reestablishment of their relationship, father and son rebuilt a closeness, based on a sense of shared responsibility for keeping the family going, companionship, football and visits to the seaside. The mutual love between them, through ups and downs, gradually grew, until six years later, with a bitter irony, his father collapsed with a stroke in the same room in which his mother had been taken ill. He began to lose his father again that day, even though he did not die for another two years. So Daniel learned early that we can lose those to whom we are close. To make himself forget about the past and the pain associated with it, he removed everything which might remind him of it. To this day he has no photographs of his parents to show his own children and virtually nothing that belonged to either of them. He wishes that someone had encouraged him then to keep a few mementos at least.

Bob's death reminded him, originally unconsciously, of the deaths of both his parents. It brought to the front of his mind how much he still missed his father. What came out of this painful awareness has been the re-evaluation of his own relationship with his children in the present. He was allowing time with them to slip down his list of priorities. That list was crowded at the top with work, work and yet more work. As a result, he talked over his long hours with his boss, who had also become something of a workaholic, and gained agreement to get home earlier at least two days a week in order to spend time with his family. He is also making opportunities to do things with his children in a way that he had previously failed to do.

Bereavement counselling is not desirable for everyone who is bereaved, but in Daniel's case it helped to disentangle the threads of three losses, spread over 20 years. Individually they were manageable, but together added up to a bewildering and what initially felt like an overwhelming mountain of grief.

His line manager was astute enough to see that counselling might help, and Daniel accepted the offer of this kind of help, because he realised that he was feeling low: his motivation and performance had dived. It also helped that he had participated in an introduction to counselling skills residential workshop for all the senior members of the human resources department a few years before. The workshop had dispelled some of his fears and suspicions about counselling, and made it less difficult for him to contemplate using the process without feeling that he was being weak.

The Farmer and His Father's Death

The four farm cottages made an excellent base for a holiday in the countryside, not far from the sea. You needed to book well in advance if you wanted to rent one during the summer. Easter and

Whitsun bookings were picking up, although they tended to be empty for most of the year. George, still active in his late 70s ran the holiday cottages as a part-time retirement job. It brought in some extra income to the farm, which was under increasing economic pressures. Their milk now fetched a third of the price of three years ago.

George was born in the farmhouse in which he still lived with his son, Richard. His wife had died five years previously six months before their golden wedding. When George started working on the farm, helping his father, there were 10 men. Now Richard did it all on his own with occasional help from one nomadic farm worker during harvest time. Working with a tractor and ear muffs was both faster and also more isolated than with the long gone team of horses.

Then one day, George had a heart attack and died.

Richard then had to contend with an isolation in his bereavement that was different to previous generations. The workplace seemed very empty. There was no human company on the farm, now that he did not have his father to argue with or consult, depending on the mood of the moment. He felt glad that he was not just an arable farmer, and found some comfort in the companionship of their animals, especially his two dogs. The vicar, based in a village 5 miles away, did his best but Richard hardly knew him. Like many of his generation, he felt alienated from the church, though his parents were involved: his mother had run the choir and been active in the Mothers' Union. He thought about going again after the funeral, but decided against it. He was busy and doubted if he believed half of what was said in the services.

In some ways, it was a relief. He was glad that both his parents had had their '3 score years and 10' and been spared debilitating final illnesses. They had both died at home, as they had wanted. Furthermore, in their case, two had seemed to make less company than three. After his mother's death, he found his father got on his nerves more than he used to. But the isolation really got to him, and he was surprised by his grief, which was greater than when his mother died. His father's death not only severed their link but also his last link with her too. So he seemed to be grieving for them both. And it was so hard doing it all on his own. He and his father never cried in front of each other when his mother died, but they talked about her a lot. There was no one to talk to now.

Richard began to feel he understood why some people killed themselves. What was the point of going on living? He had never felt like that before, and had been totally perplexed when, two years before, a neighbouring farmer took his car into the hills one day and fitted a hose to the exhaust. But Richard did not kill himself. He decided that he did have a reason to go on living, although he was not sure that he could put it into words. Slowly he worked through the bereavement process in his own way, cursing and grumbling as he got out of bed in the morning and went about keeping the farm going, rattling around in the farmhouse designed for a family. But it was the loneliness of bereavement that impacted on him with most force, because it mirrored and reinforced the increasing isolation of his workplace and community.

A Daughter's Death

It was a dense foggy evening in early December, when Ian's youngest child Nicola had her accident. She was only 24 when it happened. She and her partner had recently moved into a new home, a cottage in the country 15 miles from where she worked. Visibility that night was down to a few yards, and the lane down which they lived had no lighting or road markings. Apparently she missed her way and drove off the road into a tree. 999 was alerted by a neighbour who saw the wreck shortly afterwards, but Nicola was dead by the time that the ambulance arrived.

Ian and Nicola's mother Brenda were shaken to their roots, but somehow got through the few weeks afterward. They had been helped by the support they were able to give and, even more, receive from Nicola's partner and some of her close friends, who they had known for years. These young people spoke and made music at the funeral, and made them realise how special a human being they also thought their daughter was. They took to dropping in frequently on Ian and Brenda for endless cups of this and that round their kitchen table, when they would reminisce about Nicola. It was as if all their lives had come to a full stop. The younger generation seemed a lot less inhibited than they were, but they all had a sense of shared grief and support by maintaining contact

At work, Ian felt gutted, but relieved how well he was hacking it, at least at first, but he was worried about Brenda. She and Nicola had always had an almost telepathic relationship, and had always stayed very close. Nicola had seemed to miss out on her adolescent rebellion phase, which was mostly directed in a couple of years of struggle with her father, but even that had abated after she left home to go to college. Since then, Nicola's friendship with both parents had become relaxed as well as strong.

Ian encouraged Brenda to talk to their GP, who had put her on anti-depressants and pointed her towards a counsellor. She had some good women friends, not least at the council offices where she worked as a section leader in the housing department. Brenda's line manager encouraged her to take her time in coming back to work fully, in mind if not in body. 'I know that you are only human, so you are bound to be miles away from time to time, even if you are at your desk. So don't worry, and don't give yourself a hard time. None of us will.' She still felt emotionally battered, but did not anticipate that anything else was possible, given what had happened.

Now six moths later, Brenda felt that she was coming up for air, but things were not so good for Ian. In the aftermath of the tragedy, he had seemed strong, holding the family together, even though his work took him away from home quite a bit as it always had. He held a senior position in an advertising agency, where he had worked for 20 years, with quite a few clients based outside the UK. He had got back to work a couple of weeks after Nicola's death and assured his boss that to work normally would be the most helpful policy as far as he was concerned. His colleagues, all men and most of whom he had worked with for years, were concerned for him. But they did not really know what to say and so they got on with their work. Neither he nor they initiated conversations about his daughter's death.

His boss became increasingly worried about him. The quality of his work deteriorated and his inter-personal skills deserted him. He was more irritable than he used to be, and some of his colleagues shared their concerns about him. He had become a byword in the company for his skill and experience. In the past few months, however, he had lost some of his edge and it seemed to be getting worse. Maybe he was just running out of steam, rather than grieving over his daughter's death. He should have got over it by now ...

That was the gist of what Ian's boss shared with the Human Resources Director, who suggested that as he had had a few months to work through his bereavement, it might be useful to offer him some counselling. Ian accepted the suggestion, partly because he felt that he was sinking.

What emerged from the counselling was that he had not really talked to anybody, except Brenda, about what he was going through, certainly not his male friends, who conspired to try and cheer him up at all costs, and that was backfiring. If he refused to be cheered, they got fed up with him and he with them. Because he felt that Brenda's grief was greater than his, he minimised the latter with her (and to an extent with himself), rather than risk upsetting her more than she was already. He talked a lot with the counsellor about his family and Nicola's life and her death. What also came to the surface was how much he had missed out in terms of sheer time with her and his other children and his home during the years he had been working, with frequent trips abroad.

Work had had its own impetus and bowled him along, and he had never really stopped to think about his priorities. Her death was forcing to the surface of his mind a re-evaluation of the time and the energy he spent at home and at work. As with many other people, bereavement made Ian rethink his workaholic life and values. In his case it led to a decision nine months later to take an early retirement option, to which he was entitled. It meant some careful calculations and equally careful discussion with Brenda, because there were financial consequences in going early. He told the HR Director when sorting out the details of his departure: 'I guess we cannot have a tragedy like this happen and just steam on as if nothing had happened. It's got to me in ways I just didn't expect.' Before his daughter's death, neither Ian, Brenda or his colleagues would have imagined such a decision from him of all people.

Appendix 1
The Core Conditions of Helping

'The Core Conditions of Helping' have been identified as an excellent basis for building good relationships, teams and individual, work and non-work, without unnecessary stress. They can be easily remembered by an accessible acronym MUG: M for Mutual Respect (and acceptance), U for Understanding (and Empathy, which essentially means communicating understanding) and G for Genuineness (and honesty). They are crucial in supporting those who are bereaved or terminally ill.

Mutual respect or acceptance involves an acceptance of and respect for people as human beings, without any sense of intrinsic superiority over them on the basis of status, qualifications, race, tribe, age, gender, state of health or for any other reason. Mutual respect also implies a commitment to staff as people. If I feel that the organisation, through my manager, is committed to my health, welfare and success, I am more likely to reciprocate through my commitment to the health, welfare and success of the company through the principle of 'Do as you would be done by'.

It also requires us to remember constantly the interdependence of everyone in the organisation for its success, whatever job you happen to occupy at the moment. Such respect for the person needs to underpin and be stronger than respect for their effectiveness and output, which may be adversely affected by illness or bereavement, at least in the short term. It does not mean accepting, agreeing with or failing to challenge unacceptable behaviour or differing views to you own, nor shirking from disciplinary action, if and when required. It does mean distinguishing in your own mind and behaviour between the person you are disciplining who is as worthy of respect as you are, and their behaviour or performance, which is a cause of concern. That sense of respect may be the crucial ingredient that makes it possible for the person to respond undefensively to the points you are making, and retain enough motivation and energy to act on it constructively. Disciplinary action needs even more to be a last resort in times of bereavement than it would be in normal times.

Empathy is the ability to communicate *understanding* and to see a situation from another person's point of view. The key skills for understanding are listening and reflecting. The stereotype of leadership is one in which the leader dominates by talking, if not shouting, while the led listen: for such a leader to listen with respect to subordinates would be a sign of weakness, because the leader should also have a monopoly of wisdom. Such a model gives leadership a bad name. Listening leaders understand and respect their people and appreciate that each of them has a unique perspective on their own job, which maybe no-one else has. Their suggestions on how to do the job better and also on broader issues for the company are worth taking seriously, even if there may be reasons for not acting on all their recommendations. Such a leader does not need to be indecisive.

Effective listening is vital from a manager or supervisor, who is with a staff member coming to terms with his own or someone else's death. It is achieved through the eyes and the whole body, not just the ears, because it involves the non-verbal both ways. If you are not looking at the person while you listen, you risk giving the impression that you are not really listening whole-heartedly with interest and respect. You also risk missing some important non-verbal clues, which may add to your understanding, especially about how the person feels. Reflecting is an essential component of communicating understanding through reflecting back your sense of what the person is essentially saying and also often acknowledging how they are feeling. Too often people listen without looking and restrict their verbal inputs to questioning, without reflecting: such listening tends to be low on competence, empathy and encouragement.

Genuineness is the capacity to be straight, to be yourself and not hide behind a mask of some kind, such as your role, or to play devious games. The sense that someone is pretending to care in the face of bereavement, but actually does not give a toss is very alienating. The more genuine you are, the more likely you are to be yourself whether at home or in different work settings, rather than switching your genuineness on and off, depending on who you are with. The cost of being genuine is, by not putting up the barricades of self-protecting, false professionalism, that you too will be affected and perhaps upset as well. Another reason some find it hard to be genuine with certain people is a lack of self-confidence. Such confidence can be built in a variety of ways, depending on your particular needs: through accepting yourself, as well as other people; through assertiveness; through strengthening support; and through high quality feedback. An anxiety that prevents some leaders being genuine is the fear that their authority may be undermined by a lack of 'distance' between them and their staff; but familiarity and being genuine are not the same. While at times leadership may require detachment and objectivity in considering people and problems, they need to be combined with humanity. Honesty has been identified as the key attribute wanted by staff from their managers and also came top of the list of qualities often thought to be lacking. People want to trust their managers and to feel that they are genuine, particularly at times of personal difficulty or vulnerability. Sometimes that may mean the manager has to admit that they do not know what to say or do for the best.

The core conditions of helping complement rather than contradict the ACL (action-centred leadership) emphasis on action and doing. How we lead is as important as what we do. Max De Pree, a successful chairman of an American company, put it differently: 'Leaders owe the organisation a new reference point for what caring, purposeful, committed people can be in the institutional setting. Notice I did not say what people can do – what people can do is merely a consequence of what we can be. Corporations, like the people who compose them, are always in a state of becoming.'1 The core conditions provide an essential, sound foundation on which to build effective leadership, motivation and team work.

Note

1. DePree, Max: *Leadership is an Art* – Doubleday, New York 1989.

Appendix 2
Checklists

Please feel free to copy any of the pages that follow.

A Checklist for the Bereaved Person

If someone close to you has died, it may be helpful to know how others have coped in similar situations, even though your experience is unique. These notes draw together some important points.

1. Your feelings

The emotional pain of bereavement is very strong and unavoidable: its depth will be a reflection of how deeply you loved or cared for the person who has died. If death came after an illness which you (and perhaps the person) knew was terminal, you may already have started the process of mourning (or healing the pain of loss). But however much you imagine you are prepared for someone's death, the actual experience often makes you feel that you have not really anticipated it at all. If the person died suddenly and unexpectedly, there may be a more prolonged period of shock (when it may be hard to take in what has happened) before the grieving begins.

Normal feelings

It is usual to experience, often very strongly, a mixture of feelings, coming one after the other repeatedly, although not necessarily in this order:

- Shock and numbness
- Longing
- Sadness or depression
- Disappointment

- Anger and resentment
- Loneliness
- Fear
- Helplessness
- Guilt, shame or regret
- Hope and despair
- Happy memories
- Resignation or acceptance

2. *Your Dreams*

Even if you do not normally remember your dreams, you may now recall very vivid dreams, perhaps bad ones. They may make a lot of sense, or not much at all. These dreams are a method by which the unconscious mind works over the feeling mentioned in the previous section, sorting them out while the conscious part of the mind is at rest.

3. *Your Body's Response*

Your body responds to bereavement as well. You may frequently experience such physical sensations as:

- Sleeplessness
- Breathing difficulties
- Headaches and other discomfort
- Tiredness
- Dizziness
- Diarrhoea and nausea
- Difficulty in concentrating and remembering things

If you are concerned about any of these symptoms, it may be helpful to consult your GP and make sure that you mention your bereavement.

4. *The Healing Process*

Your body, mind and 'heart' need to be healed from the shock and pain of your loss. This happens naturally, if you let it and allow yourself time. The quality of support you receive from family and friends is important: sometimes the healing process needs others present as you work through your feelings, although sometimes you may want to be alone.

Sharing your feelings with another person who is not too

closely involved can be very helpful, since you will feel less obliged to protect them from how you are really feeling. This is why bereavement counselling can be so valuable.

It your pain heals, it does not mean that you did not care enough in the first place. If you loved the person deeply, there will always be a gap in your heart. What healing means is that you start to be able to feel normal again, and to feel whole, without the person. This may mean that you have begun to take something of their quality and personality into your own life.

Emotional healing happens through:

- Allowing yourself to 'feel the feelings', and to share how you feel with a trusted person. You will want to think and talk about what you particularly treasure about the person who has died, the relationship you had and your memories of times together, both happy and sad.
- Being prepared to do this thinking and talking again and again. It may seem like repetition, but it is never quite the same and this kind of healing needs a lot of time.
- Being prepared to let your body 'feel the feelings' as well as your mind. You can do this through talking with feeling or passion, through laughing, crying, raging, shaking and yawning. Don't bottle up your feelings or stop your body from doing those things. Let your body express itself, when and where it feels safe to do so, on your own and also with people you trust.

5. Time-Scales

How long will it take? Talk about time-scales for 'recovery' is often avoided because every bereavement is unique and generalisations are therefore difficult. But two points can be emphasised:

- Mourning someone close to you is not a short-term process. The overwhelming aspects of acute grief may loosen their grip intermittently after a few days, but the full process can take months, even years. A sign of moving forward is the re-occurrence of periods when you feel more normal, even like you used to feel. When painful feelings return, however, they can often be as intense as ever.
- If after a few weeks you still feel constantly overwhelmed by extreme grief, it may help to consult someone, if you have not already done so: for example, a counsellor, your local branch of CRUSE, the Gay Bereavement Project, your family doctor, the Samaritans or someone at the local church.

Don't be surprised, however, if at times you still feel devastated long after the person has died. Poignant memories and reminders – visits to old haunts, photographs, letters, birthdays, Christmas and other anniversaries – can all trigger a sense of acute grief. Some people get worried if they still feel low a couple of weeks after a bereavement, but the process of mourning doesn't come to an end when compassionate leave is over and you return to work.

6. Others Who Are Grieving

If there are other people also deeply affected by the loss, it may help them if you find out how they are feeling. There is a measure of healing simply in good listening, with discretion and free from the fear of gossip.

This is especially important for children: they grieve too and will need to talk and sometimes to express their feelings through games and drawings. If you are a parent, let your children share in your grief too. If they are not aware of it because you are shielding them from it, they may feel that you don't care, and they can feel cut off from their own grief.

7. Safety

Because bereavement affects levels of stress and tiredness, you will need to watch yourself and others with respect to safety at home and work. In particular, drive carefully. Warn children to be careful, and be less inclined than usual to blame them if they do have an accident. They need extra support too, like yourself.

Be careful if you are increasing your consumption of alcohol or nicotine. Apart from the safety implications, they will not actively assist the healing process, and can even impede it. They may numb painful feelings for a short time, but not for long.

8. Practicalities

Allow yourself more time than usual to do things at home and work. Be more prepared than usual to accept offers of help, including matters relating to the bereavement. These may include:

- Registering the death
- Letting people know
- Decisions:
  - where the body should be
  - cremation or burial
  - where the ashes should go
- Funeral arrangements
- Letters and callers
- Pension, insurance and other financial matters
- Personal possessions

But give yourself time over decisions. It is often best to defer major decisions about the future if that is possible. It is no time to hurry unless it is really essential.

9. Work

Consider your colleagues as potential resources for emotional and practical help. If they offer help, either accept it or at least do not automatically refuse; take the telephone number and be prepared to call them, if you feel the offer was genuine. If colleagues can help, they act as a bridge between you and the workplace. It may be important to have such a bridge in place after a bereavement.

If you have not already done so, arrange to meet your supervisor before you return to work or as soon as possible on returning, so that you can talk things over.

Take as much time off work as you feel you need and are permitted. If your compassionate leave allowance seems inadequate, talk it over with your line manager and/or someone in personnel or welfare, or your trades union representative. If, after that, you still feel that you need more time, discuss it with your GP who may decide to 'sign you off' for a while.

Pace your return to work in consultation with your supervisor. Here are two practical suggestions:

- It may be possible to return initially on a part-time basis, say for the first week or two.
- Recognise that your concentration and capacity for creative thought will be below par at first. Some relatively easy, undemanding work may be a good way of easing you back in.

If you have someone at work whom you can trust, continue well after the bereavement to talk to this person about how it is going for you.

Remember that some painful feelings may return, long after the bereavement, as powerful and as devastating as ever. This does not mean that you are failing to make progress. At times grieving can feel a bit like going around in circles; but accepting, and going with it, is the way through. What it probably suggests is that you need to complete one more bit of grieving, and that you are ready to do so.

How to Support People During Bereavement: For Friends, Relatives and Neighbours

- Encourage them to talk about the person who has died and how they died.
- Share your own memories of the person who has died.
- Enable people to cry without loss of safety or self-respect.
- Encourage them to talk about the support (or lack of it) – good and bad – which they are receiving.
- Make early morning telephone calls and give permission to telephone during the night.
- Give practical help or teaching tasks which the deceased previously did, e.g. cooking or car maintenance.
- Revisiting old haunts – encouraging them, asking how it was and/or accompanying them.
- Encouragement to take up new interests, make new friends etc. – when the time is right.
- Discouragement from taking major decisions, e.g. house moves, remarriage, job changes etc., during the first few months of bereavement.
- Be around after the funeral and immediate period of mourning, when family and friends tend to disappear.
- Be aware of danger signals, e.g. prolonged anorexia, heavy drinking, withdrawal etc., which indicate the need for more expert help.
- Reassurance that realistic dreams, talking to the deceased, forgetting not to lay his or her place at the dinner table etc., are all quite normal – there is enormous fear of insanity at this time.
- Remembering anniversaries (e.g. death, birthday, wedding) and finding a way of acknowledging them.
- Provide companionship at work and/or outside.

Appendix 3
Further Reading

Death and bereavement has been written about extensively from many angles: this is a selection.

Anthologies

Albery, Nicholas, Elliot, Gil and Elliot, Joseph eds *The New Natural Death Handbook* (Rider, London, 1997)

Saunders, Cicely *Beyond All Pain*: *a companion for the suffering and bereaved* (SPCK, London, 1983)

Whitaker, A. (ed.), *All in the End is Harvest*: *An Anthology for Those Who Grieve* (DLT/Cruse, London, 1984)

Death and Bereavement – general

Ainsworth-Smith, Ian and Speck, Peter *Letting Go*: *Caring for the Dying and Bereaved* (SPCK, London 1982)

Charles-Edwards, A. *The Nursing Care of the Dying Patient*, (Beaconsfield Publishers, Beaconsfield 1983)

De Hennezel, M. *Intimate Death*: *how the dying teach us to live*, (Little, Brown and Company, London 1997)

Dickenson, Donna and Johnson, Malcolm (eds) *Death, Dying & Bereavement* (Sage Publications with the Open University, 1993)

Hinton, J. *Dying* (Pelican, Harmondsworth, 1967)

Kubler-Ross, E. *On Death and Dying* (Tavistock, London, 1973)

Lake, T. *Living with Grief* London, Sheldon, 1984

Nutall, D *The Early Days of Grieving* (Beaconsfield, Beaconsfield Publishers, 1991)

Parks, C.M. *Bereavement*: *Studies of Grief in Adult Life* Harmondsworth, Pelican, 1975

Raphael, B. *The Anatomy of Bereavement* (Hutchinson, London, 1982)
   Poss, S. *Towards Death with Dignity* (Allen & Unwin, London, 1981)

Raphael, B. *The Anatomy of Bereavement* London, Hutchinson, London, 1982)

Stedeford, A. *Facing Death*: *Patients, Families and Professionals* (Heinemann Medical, London, 1984)

Tatelbaum, J. *The Courage to Grieve*, London Heinemann, 1981

Worden, W. *Grief Counselling and Grief Therapy*, (Tavistock, London, 1983)

Bereavement, Relationships and the Family

Pincus, L. *Death and the Family: The Importance of Mourning*, (Faber, London, 1976)

Shuchter, Stephen R. *Dimensions of Grief: adjusting to the death of a spouse* (Jossey-Bass, London, 1986)

Staudacher, Carol *Men & Grief*, (New Harbinger Publications, Oakland, CA, USA, 1991)

Bereavement and Children

Black, Dora et al. *Father Kills Mother: Post-Traumatic Stress Disorder in the Children* (Bereavement Care: Cruse, London, Spring 1993)

Bowlby, John *Attachment and loss: Loss, sadness and depression* (Basic Books, New York, 1980)

Dominica, Sister Frances *Just My Reflection: helping parents to do things their way when their child dies* (DLT, London, 1997)

Jewett, Claudia, *Helping Children Cope with Separation and Loss* Childcare Policy and Practice (B.T.Batsford, London, 1982)

Merrington, Bill *Suffering Love: Coping with the death of a child*, (Advantage, Leamington Spa, Warwickshire 1996)

Worden, W. *Children and Grief*, (Guldford Press, New York and London, 1996)

Personal Accounts of Bereavement and Dying

Blacker, Terence *The spirituality of sad old hippies* (The Independent, London 15 December 1998)

De Beauvoir, Simone *A Very Easy Death* (André Deutsch and Weidenfeld and Nicolson, London 1995)

Dodson, James *Final Rounds: father, son, the golf journey of a lifetime* (Arrow Books, London 1997)

Lewis, C.S. *A Grief Observed*, (Faber & Faber, London, 1961)

Parry, Colin & Wendy, *Tim: An Ordinary Boy* (Hodder and Stoughton, 1994)

Bereavement, Death, Culture and Religion

Baynes, Akemi *What happens when we die?* (UK Express, The Buddhism of Nichiren Daishonin, Taplow Court, Berkshire SL6 0ER, UK, January 1992)

Collins, David, Tank, Manju and Basith, Abdul *Concise Guide to Customs of Minority Ethnic Religions*, (Portsmouth Diocesan Council for Social Responsibility, 1992)

Gersie, Alida *Storymaking in Bereavement: dragons fight in the meadow* (Jessica Kingsley Publishers, London, 1991)

Gorer, Geoffrey *Death, Grief and Mourning*, (Crescent, London, 1965)

Laungani, Pittu *Death and Bereavement Across Cultures* (Routledge, London 1997)

Parks, Colin Murray, Laungani, Pittu and Young, Bill (eds.) *Death and Bereavement Across Cultures*, (Routledge, London, 1996)

Smart, N. 'Death in the Judaeo-Christian Tradition', *in Man's Concern with Death*, A. Toynbee et al., (Hodder & Stoughton, London, 1968)

Von Franz, Marie-Louise *On Dreams and Death, a Jungian interpretation* (Shamhala, Boston & London, 1986)

Suicide and Euthanasia

Davies, Jean (foreword by Dirk Bogarde), *Choice in Dying: the facts about voluntary euthanasia* (Ward Lock, London, 1997)

The Samaritans, *The Cost of Stress*, (The Samaritans 10 The Grove, Slough, SL1 1QP, 1996)

The Samaritans, *Listen Up: responding to people in crisis*, (The Samaritans 10 The Grove, Slough, SL1 1QP, 1998)

The Samaritans, *Exploring the taboo: attitudes of young people towards suicide and depression*, (The Samaritans 10 The Grove, Slough, SL1 1QP, 1997)

The Samaritans *Challenging the taboo: attitudes towards suicide and depression*, (The Samaritans 10 The Grove, Slough, SL1 1QP, 1996)

Wertheimer, Alison *A Special Scar: the experience of people bereaved by suicide* (Routledge, London 1991)

The Advance Directive: information is available from The Voluntary Euthanasia Society, 13 Prince of Wales Terrace, London W8 5PG (0207 937 7770)

People and Work: Counselling and Helping Skills

Adams, Andrea *Bullying at Work* (Virago, London, 1992)

Feltham, Colin (editor) *The Gains of Listening: Perspectives on Counselling at Work* (Open University Press, Buckingham, 1997)

Mackay, Ian *Listening Skills* in the Management Shapers series (Institute of Personnel and Development, London, 1998)

Moores, R, *Managing For High Performance*, (The Industrial Society, London, 1994)

Murgatoyd, Steve & Woolfe, Ray *Coping with Crisis: Understanding and Helping People in Need*, (Harper & Row, London, 1982)

Reddy, Michael *The Manager's Guide to Counselling at Work* (British Psychological Society and Methuen, London 1987)

Reddy, Michael (ed.) *EAPs and Counselling Provision in UK Organisations*, (Independent Counselling and Advisory Service, Milton Keynes, 1993)

Ryan, Kathleen D. & Oestreich, Daniel K. *Driving Fear Out Of The Workplace* (Jossey-Bass Publishers, San Francisco, 1991)

Stewart, William *An A-Z of Counselling Theory and Practice* (Chapman & Hall, London 1992)

Thorne, B. (editor), *Symposium: Spiritual Dimensions in Counselling* (British Journal of Guidance & Counselling, Vol.18, No.3), Cambridge, Hobson Publishing, September 1990

Appendix 4

Organisations Supporting the Bereaved

Asian Family Counselling Service, Equity Chamber 2nd Floor, 40 Piccadilly, Bradford BD1 3NN (01274 720486).

British Humanist Association, 14 Lamb's Conduit Passage, London, WC1R 4RH (0207- 43- 0908). Provides help with non-religious funerals.

Cancerlink, 11-21 Northdown Street, London N1 9BN.

Cancer Helpline 0800 132 905, Asian Helpline 0800 500 415.

MAC Helpline (young people) 0800 591 028.

The Compassionate Friends, 53 North Street, Bristol BS3 1EN (0117 953 9639). Support offered to bereaved parents by other bereaved parents. Special groups for those in the shadow of suicide and for parents of murdered children. Contact nationally for local telephone number. Area served: 80 branches throughout UK.

Cot Death Research and Support for Bereaved Parents, 8a Alexandra Parade, Weston-Super-Mare BS23 1TQ (0836 219010 / 09234 613333 / 0934 413333) A counselling service to newly-bereaved parents and their families following the unexpected death of their baby. Area served: UK.

CRUSE-Bereavement Care, 126 Sheen Road, Richmond, Surrey TW9 1UR (0208-332 7227) Counselling advice on practical problems and opportunities for social contact for all bereaved people. For local branch information, contact CRUSE nationally. Area served: UK.

The Elizabeth Kubler-Ross Foundation – Friends of Shanti Nilaya UK, PO Box 212, London NW8 7NW. Offers a series of lectures and workshops, including 'Life, Death and Transition' an intensive course for up to 90 people from a variety of backgrounds as well as terminally ill patients and the parents of terminally ill children.

Foundation for the Study of Infant Deaths (SIDS) – Cot Death Research And Support), 14 Halkin Street, London SW1X 7DP (0207-235 1721) Cot Death Helpline 0207 235 0965. Gives personal support to bereaved families offering a befriending service.

Lesbian and Gay Bereavement Project, Vaughan M Williams Centre, Colindale Hospital, London NW9 5HG (0208-455 8894) or via Gay switchboard (0207-837 7324). Telephone support and counselling to those bereaved by loss of same sex partner.

Jewish Bereavement Counselling Service PO Box 6748, London N3 3BX (0181-349 0839).

London Bereavement Projects Group, c/o London Voluntary Service, 68 Chalton Street, Camden Town, London NW1 1JR (0207-388 2153). Bereaved people can contact the group to find the name of a local group for bereavement counselling. Offers support, training and guidelines to all London Bereavement Services. Area Served: Greater London.

National Association of Bereavement Services, 20 Norton Folgate, London E1 6DB (0207-247 0617). A nationwide network of organisations and individuals offering services to bereaved people and also a Helpline (0207-247 1080) for those who are bereaved: 10-4 Monday to Friday to provide information about your nearest, most appropriate source of support.

Person to Person, 5 Mountside, Stanmore, Harrow HA7 2DS (0208-422 8045). General addiction, bereavement and marital counselling. Training and consultation. Area served: NW London, Herts and Bucks.

RoadPeace, the national charity for road traffic victims, PO Box 2579, London NW10 3PW (advice and help line 0208 964 1021. Established in 1992 to respond to the need for an organisation supporting road traffic victims, drawing attention to their lack of rights and the disregard of their needs and campaigning for real road safety.

Stillbirth and Neonatal Death Society (SANDS), 28 Portland Place, London W1N 4DE (0207-436 5881). Help to individuals or couples by way of befriending or group support from parents who have suffered a similar bereavement.

Sudden Death Support Association, Chapel Green House, Wokingham, Berkshire RG40 3ER (01189 790790). Supporting the relatives and close friends of those who die suddenly.

Support after Murder and Manslaughter (SAMM), Cranmer House, 39 Brixton Road, London SW9 3DZ (0207-735 9166).

Survivors of Bereavement by Suicide (SOBS), 82 Arcon Drive, Anlaby Road, Hull HU4 6AD (01482 565387).

Terence Higgins Trust, BM Aids, London WC1N 3XX (0207 242 1010). Information and support for those who are concerned that they may be HIV Positive or have AIDS.

The Child Bereavement Trust, Brindley House, 4 Burkes Road, Beaconsfield, Bucks HP9 1PB, telephone: 01494 678 088.

Winston's Wish: A Grief Support Programme for Children, founded in 1992. Gloucestershire Hospital, Great Western Road, Gloucester GL1 3NN, telephone: 01452 394 377.

Some of these and other organisations are listed in the Counselling & Psychotherapy Resources Directory, produced periodically by the *British Association for Counselling* (BAC), 1 Regent Place, Rugby CV21 2PJ (01788 578328).

Index